Women CROSSING BORDERS

Reflections on Cross-cultural Ministry

Cheri Pierson
Editor

emis

Evangelism and Missions
Information Service

BILLY GRAHAM CENTER
WHEATON COLLEGE

Women Crossing Borders:
Reflections on Cross-cultural Ministry

Cheri Pierson, editor

Published by EMIS, a division of the Billy Graham Center, Wheaton College, Wheaton, Ill.

Cover design and layout: Dona Diehl
Cover photos courtesy IMB

Printed in the United States of America.

For information about other publications of EMIS:
P.O. Box 794, Wheaton, IL 60189
Email: emis@wheaton.edu
Website: www.billygrahamcenter.org/emis

For information about the Billy Graham Center:
500 College Ave., Wheaton, IL 60187
Email: bgcadm@wheaton.edu
Website: www.billygrahamcenter.org

ISBN 1-879089-39-4

#294997937

ENDORSEMENTS

. . . .

"In an unsettled and dangerous world, it takes courage and a clear sense of ministry for Christian women to respond to a missionary calling. Wheaton Graduate School has trained hundreds of exceptional missionaries who are now making outstanding and faithful contributions to the spread of the gospel. Cheri's book captures some of their amazing experiences, told in their own words. These are amusing, touching, insightful and sometimes almost miraculous accounts of how they have seen the work of the Lord."

—*Dr. Myrna Grant, author, professor emeritus, Wheaton College*

. . . .

"The real stories shared within these pages by women in the trenches of mission work will both inspire and challenge you. These women learned to trust God for that which seemed unlikely, improbable, even impossible."

—*Dr. Pamela Trice, counselor*

. . . .

"While reading the stories of *Women Crossing Borders* I was struck at the extraordinarily particular and often uncommonly surprising ways in which God meets his daughters at places of need as they serve him. These vignettes cause one to reflect anew on 'the God who sees me.' An inspiring book."

—*Evvy Hay Campbell, associate professor of Intercultural Studies, Wheaton College*

DEDICATION

. . . .

For Bri

Brianna Esswein (2005), a former student of mine, went home to be with Jesus Christ on December 11, 2005, when she and seven others with Youth with a Mission were killed in a tragic road accident outside Port Hourcourt, Nigeria. Her twenty-five years were lived with energetic zeal, vibrant faith and endless passion to serve her Lord. The following portion taken from a letter she wrote just four days before her accident expresses her commitment:

He has called me to a life of both joy and suffering. I am willing to live and die for my Lord and will follow him to the ends of the earth, knowing that it may cost me everything, but that there is no greater joy than serving my God and only through him can my life and my joy be made complete.

May Bri's example and the women represented in this book encourage others to cross borders for Christ and his kingdom.

CONTENTS

FOREWORD 9
ACKNOWLEDGEMENTS 12
INTRODUCTION 13

ALBANIA
When investing in others
Ana — *Lynette Holm Hoppe* 17

BANGLADESH
When something seems impossible
Little Nudgy Finds a Home — *Beth Tebbe* 20

BOLIVIA
When facing opposition
Women Facing Opposition in Ministry – *Francesca Crane* 23

BORNEO
When searching for someone
A Trip Worth Making – *Christy Reed* 26

CHILE
When facing danger
Shipwrecked – *Shura Facanha* 30

CHINA
When finances are limited
The Christmas Violin – *Ming* 34

EAST AFRICA
When turning evil to good
A God Who Uses the Broken – *Anne* 37

EASTERN EUROPE
When traditions open up opportunities
A Lesson from a Muslim Holiday Tradition – *Clara* 40

ECUADOR
When facing disappointment
Hindsight Is 20/20 – *Youngchu Song* 43

FIJI ISLANDS
When the cost is extreme
Counting the Cost – *Becky DeBerry Bryant* 46

HUNGARY
When searching for truth
Released from Captivity – *Melody Scott* 49

INDIA
When you sense failure
Flowers in a Wall – *Sheri Lazarus* 53

INDONESIA
When facing painful memories
Reflections from a Copra Boat – *Cara Hurley* 56

JAPAN
When patience is required
Cultivating the Gift of Patient Enduring – *Holly Ann Bell* 59

KAZAKHSTAN
When you open up to someone
Marina and Fish – *Paige Buzbee Pushkin* 63

KENYA
When listening to the words of the wise
Grandpa Isindeli – *Barbara Miner Collins* 66

LIBERIA
When unexpected opportunities arise
Unexpected Windows of Opportunity – *Ruth Maxwell* 68

MEXICO
When you have to wait
Waiting for Mr. Right – *Tracey Moore Pieters* 72

MIDDLE EAST
When darkness breaks
Aisha – *Mary* 75

MONGOLIA
When actions speak louder than words
The Power of Laughter – *Kristy McGarvey* 78

MOROCCO
When being is enough
Roses to Smell – *Kimberly Wenger Sanford* 81

PAKISTAN
When the Spirit leads
The Passenger – *Ginny Feldman* 84

PAPUA NEW GUINEA
When your faith is tested
Restrictions – *Sarita Dolores Gallagher* 87

PHILIPPINES
When adopting children across cultures
Becoming a Family – *Nancy Kelley Alvarez* 90

ROMANIA
When facing a fearful situation
Helping Hands – *Jennifer Hobday* 93

RUSSIA
When called to give an answer
The Hope That We Have – *Lisa Christian* 96

SIERRA LEONE
When you least expect it
A Father Who Knows What You Need – *Evvy Campbell* 99

SOUTH AFRICA & SWAZILAND
When the task is overwhelming
Turning the Tide—Is It Possible? – *Brenda Bagley* 102

SWEDEN
When the unexpected happens
An Unexpected Friendship – *Cheri Pierson* 105

THAILAND
When making disciples across cultures
Yes, Lord – *Dorothy Mainhood* 108

TRINIDAD
When you wonder why
Why, God? – *Diane Garvin* 111

UNITED STATES
When home is far away
Where Is My Home? – *Mary Cerutti* 114

UNITED STATES
When looking for direction
Leaning In and Pressing On – *Brooke Peters* 117

UNITED STATES
When others are hurting
The Spirit's Song of Healing – *Heather Pancake* 120

UNITED STATES
When you move beyond your comfort zone
Sarah – *Dawn Herzog Jewell* 123

ZAMBIA
When risks are inevitable
We Will Fear No Evil – *Shelli Martin and Holly VanSciver* 127

FOREWORD

. . . .

Miriam Adeney

In the confusing world of the twenty-first century, many people draw small maps and stay within fixed boundaries. The office, the church, the mall, the gym, a few cafes. Janet is a friend of mine who doesn't read the newspaper anymore. Why? She says the news disturbs her, and surely God doesn't want her to be disturbed. Another friend, Maureen, confides, "Whenever I think of those people over there in that poor country, I worry. And I know God doesn't want me to be worried. So I've decided he doesn't want me to think about them."

This is not so of the women in this book. These women know the earth is the Lord's. All of Scripture rings with that message. God's concern for global issues didn't begin when Jesus said, "Go into all the world" or "You shall be my witnesses." Thousands of years earlier, Abraham heard God call his name, saying, "I will bless you...all peoples on earth will be blessed through you" (Gen. 12: 2,3). Isaiah saw the people of God as a light to the nations (49:6). Habakkuk saw the "earth filled with the knowledge of the glory of the Lord as the waters cover the sea" (2:14). Micah saw that "his greatness will reach to the ends of the earth. And he will be their peace" (5:4-5). Jonah, Daniel, Esther, Nehemiah and even Naaman's slave girl resonate with God's absorbing interest in the whole earth.

Committed women know that we cannot be healthy Christians and ignore the world. A global concern is not optional. It comes from the heart of God.

To this commission, the women in this book bring trained minds. They believe that study shows us more of the mind of God. All the chemical, psychological and astronomical processes hang together because they flow from a single mind—our Father's. So as we explore the universe rationally, probing its patterns, we are in a small way thinking God's thoughts after him. When we study science we are moved to worship.

When we draw, play music or invent, we create. In our own awkward way, we imitate God, the great Creator, who made us creative in his image. As A.A. Stockdale has said, "When God made the earth, he could have finished it. But he didn't."

He left it as raw material—to tease us, tantalize us and set us thinking, experimenting, risking and adventuring. And therein we find our supreme interest in living.

He left the music unsung and the dramas unplayed. He left the poetry undreamed, in order that men and women might not become bored, but engaged in stimulating, exciting, creative activities that keep them thinking, working, experimenting and experiencing all the joys and satisfactions of achievement.

Of course our awareness of truth is untidy. Systems are not simple; facts are not value-free. Individuals are not autonomous. Cultures are not neatly ranked. Ideals in real life are ragged. We are torn by wrenching ambiguities. Why genocide? Why incest? Why Christian ugliness? Why layoffs?

Nevertheless, even though we don't have all the answers, babies will be born, and must be raised with joy, consistency and morals. Jobs must be created. Ecological pollution must be tackled. Health care, hunger and homelessness must be faced. Nuclear proliferation in a world bristling with racial, ethnic and religious hatreds will continue to exist. In the midst of this, *people need the good news of God in Jesus.* It is in Jesus, and uniquely in Jesus, that people find their deepest hungers met, find the surest prescription for health and wholeness, find their roots and their wings.

Women who cross borders know this. But they also do more. When faced with hungry people, they try to provide food. When faced with sick people, they try to alleviate illness. They do not stay in ivory towers teaching theology, unaware of human need. Women's ministry must always be holistic, involving mind and body. Women's mission work historically has been characterized by vulnerability, nurturance, interdependence, holism and immersion in life narratives. And in the middle of the mess of real life, as women of different cultures have worked together, laughed together and cried together, sisterhood has bonded them. These are the stories of women who cross borders because they love God with all their minds so that they can love their neighbors as themselves. These are the stories of women who vibrate for Christ and his kingdom.

Miriam Adeney, whose doctorate is in anthropology, is currently associate professor of global and urban ministries at Seattle Pacific University. She is a prolific writer (Daughters of Islam) and speaker. She is also a graduate of Wheaton College.

ACKNOWLEDGEMENTS

. . . .

This devotional book required the support and cooperation of many people. I would like to thank my husband, Steve, and two sons, Jonathan and David, who continue to support and encourage me in my writing endeavors. I would also like to thank the staff of the Billy Graham Center for their part in its production.

Special thanks to Dr. Kenneth Gill who shared in the vision of this project and to Dotsey Welliver and Laurie Fortunak who edited and prepared the manuscript for publication. Many thanks to Dr. Myrna Grant who guided me through the early stages of this project, discussed ideas over warm cups of tea and read all the stories in great depth. Special thanks to my Wheaton students, Francesca Crane, Anitra Shaw, Mary Cerutti and Meg Smith who worked diligently in developing the database, contacting people and gathering information. Finally, I am indebted to Melody Scott who put many hours in editing the stories and researching information on the country backgrounds.

It goes without saying that it would have been impossible to produce this book without the women who contributed the stories from their ministries and from their hearts. I also want to thank the students in my recent Perspectives on Gender and Leadership classes at Wheaton College who have submitted stories that are not found in this volume. They also provided valuable feedback on the stories selected for this work. My thanks go to all of them and to those who daily cross borders for Christ and his kingdom.

INTRODUCTION

. . . .

Mary Magdalene was there. She personally encountered the mercy of Christ, her Deliverer.[1] She was there at the tomb, where Christ was buried.[2] Maybe it was there when Jesus called her name, that a memory was triggered. A memory of the first time the Son of God had spoken her name–that initial moment she heard the voice of mercy. When a person has a genuine experience with the mercy of God, he or she doesn't forget it. In fact, the mercy of God invokes a passion in his followers; a passion to proclaim what has been experienced.

Jesus chose to appear to women first even though their testimony was met with doubt.[3] His mercy and mandate crossed the social border of gender. Mercy invoked a passion, and passion begat proclamation. No social, economic, geographical or cultural border could stop this proclamation of the good news of Jesus Christ. Since the time Jesus gave Mary Magdalene the charge to go and tell the disciples that he was alive, countless women have been motivated by their passion to proclaim this encounter with the mercy of God.[4] Women have a long history of proclaiming Christ; and thus, as captured in this title, have crossed many kinds of borders to do so.

In the early Church women such as Lydia, Priscilla and Dorcus labored for the gospel; women worked as partners with men as well as independently in order to spread the gospel to the nations.[5] However, women continued to face difficulties. During the years after the early Church women such as Perpetua and Santa Lucia were martyred for their love for Christ. Nevertheless, women used their resources and circumstances to continue passionately proclaiming the love and mercy of Christ. In the Goth invasion of Rome in 410 A.D., women were taken as captives, but they evangelized their captors.[6] In the thirteenth century, Clare founded the Franciscan Order of nuns who cared for the poor and spread Christianity. In the Catholic tradition, women established hospitals and orphanages within the limits of their cloister and framework. By the mid-twentieth century, women were permitted to engage in full foreign mission.

Within the Protestant tradition, the Reformation changed the role of women in the Church by emphasizing that their primary role was as wives and mothers. Ruth Tucker suggested that this more restricted role within the institution of the Church led to women being drawn to the less restricted role of mission work.[7] During the nineteenth century Protestant advance in missions, women served in missions as wives and mothers. In addition to caring for their husbands and families, women were gradually integrated into the work of reaching national women in countries where men served as missionaries.

As time progressed it became apparent that they were overcommitted and needed assistance. Single women were then sent to them to help care for the children and households. However, single women soon realized their call to missions as a vocation. [In 1827, Cynthia Farrar became the first single woman sent overseas by an American agency as an assistant missionary to supervise a school for girls.[8]]

It would only be a short time before women's missionary societies sent out single women as educators, medical workers, evangelists, Bible translators and trainers of national women.[9] These societies allowed qualified women to become deeply involved in world missions and paved the way for future women to be commissioned. In addition, the women's missionary societies, which would eventually form larger mission agencies, helped support educational institutions that trained women for world missions. For example, Mary Lyon opened Mount Holyoke in 1837 which led to the formation of other mission training schools for women.[10] In 1900, approximately fifty-seven percent of the nearly six thousand American Protestant foreign missionaries were women.[11]

By the second half of the twentieth century, not only did women make up the majority of the mission force, both Catholic and Protestant, but they also constituted the majority of the global Church.[12] In the twenty-first century women stand at the door of diverse cultures postured for an unprecedented impact in announcing God's Kingdom to the global community.

Wheaton College is committed to training men and women to proclaim the gospel of Jesus Christ. Wheaton College has equipped numerous women in sharing Christ: Elisabeth Howard Elliot, the American lecturer, author and missionary to Ecuador is one example. After graduating from Wheaton College in 1948, Elisabeth went to Ecuador. In 1953, she married Jim Elliot and joined him among the Quichua Indians.[13] In 1956, Jim and four companions were speared to death in an attempt to reach Auca Indians. In 1958, Elisabeth and her three-year-old daughter, Valerie, with Rachael Saint went by invitation to live among the Aucas, where she learned the language and began translation work.[14] Even today, Elisabeth remains a popular speaker and writer of dozens of books which have stimulated interest in missions.[15]

Throughout its history, Wheaton College has maintained a strong focus on missions. In 1965, Dr. H. Wilbert Norton strengthened the emphasis on graduate training for missions. In 1983, Wheaton College Graduate School offered a concentration in Missions and Intercultural Studies with Dr. John Gration as the coordinator.[16] This graduate program has equipped many women over the years for cross-cultural ministry. These women have crossed borders because they, like Mary Magdalene, have encountered the mercy of God. Christ has called them to go and tell of his Kingdom. This devotional book documents numerous inspirational and compelling stories of Wheaton women who have carried the message of Christ to the nations. The purpose of this book is to share their stories so readers will be challenged to pray for them in their work as well as broaden our own vision for Christ's Kingdom. This book gives voice to their contributions in holistic mission as they cross borders and proclaim Christ.

Endnotes

1. Luke 8:2
2. Mark 16:1-2; Luke 24:1-10; John 20:1-18
3. Mark 16:11; Luke 24:11
4. Mark 16:10
5. Acts 16:14-15,40 ; Rom.16:3-5; 2 Tim.4:19
6. Kraft, Marguerite. 2000. "Women in Missions." In A. Scott Moreau ed. *Evan-*

gelical Dictionary of World Missions. Grand Rapid, Mich.: Baker Books, 1021.

7. Tucker, Ruth. 1988. *Guardians of the Great Commission: The Story of Women in Modern Missions*. Grand Rapdis, Mich.: Zondervan Publishing House, 9.

8. Kraft, Marguerite. 2000.

9. Ibid.

10. Ibid.

11. Roberts, Dana. 2002. *Gospel Bearers, Gender Barriers: Missionary Women in the Twentieth Century*. MaryKnoll, N.Y.: Orbis Books, 5.

12. Howard, David M. 2001. *From Wheaton to the Nations*. Chicago, Ill.: Wheaton College, 20.

13. Elliot, Elisabeth. 1958. *Shadow of the Almighty*. San Francisco, Calif.: Harper & Row Publishers.

14. Howard, David M. 2000. "Elisabeth Howard Elliot." In A. Scott Moreau, ed. *Evangelical Dictionary of World Missions*. Grand Rapid, Mich.: Baker Books, 308-309.

15. Ibid.

16. Howard, David M. 2000, 108.

ALBANIA

When investing in others

. . . .

Ana

Lynette Holm Hoppe

The land of Albania is as diverse as the religions and cultures of its people. From the rugged mountains to the Adriatic coastlines, the beauty of the land mesmerizes. The magnificent inland lakes and natural lagoons make up for the fact that this country ranks as one of the smallest and poorest countries in Europe. Albania's transition to democracy in the 1990s ended its 42-year communist reign. Today, Albania has a growing Muslim population.

Scripture – I Thessalonians 1:2-3

We always thank God for all of you, mentioning you in our prayers. We continually remember before our God and Father your work produced by faith, your labor prompted by love and your endurance inspired by hope in our Lord Jesus Christ.

Story

Many teenage girls do not have an opportunity to receive solid Christian teaching at home. In a unique way, camp offers an opportunity by surrounding the girls with people who know Christ and hope to bring others into a deeper relationship with him. Faith Veronis had taken upon herself the responsibility of training this year's camp leadership. Although each day overflowed with activity, including morning and evening prayers, Bible studies, special speakers, crafts, sporting events and more, the program rested entirely in the hands of three young women from our seminary. All of them proved worthy to take command, but I would like to highlight one of the young directors, a woman named Ana Baba.

Although she came from humble beginnings in a village near Fier, Albania, she graduated head and shoulders above her classmates at the Resurrection of Christ Theological Academy. Ana became this year's valedictorian. She is the fourth child in the Baba family to graduate from that school; she was preceded by two older brothers and a sister, who was salutatorian last year. Only her zeal and love for Christ exceeds her brilliance as a student. Always ready and willing to work hard, she excelled in academic work, camp leadership, catechism, evangelism and any other duty assigned.

It became clear that God was preparing her for her greatest desire—to be a missionary in Albania, and any other place where the gospel has not been preached. In all my interactions with young Ana, her ability to bear witness to Christ stood out. What I noticed most about her, however, was not her learned speech or exceptional skills, but her ready smile. It always lit up with joy, gentleness and humility.

Ana's desire to reach her own people with the gospel is not an easy task. The spiritual and social needs of Albania sometimes seem overwhelming. Many poor and desperate people come to our own doors each day. But young women like Ana exist—those who stand ready and willing to be equipped and sent out. All they need is enough grace to learn discernment and love, so that they might best know how to bring the gospel to people in Jesus' name.

Journaling Topic

How would you build bridges to people from an Orthodox background, like Albanians? What advice would you give in helping the "poor and desperate people" who came to the Hoppes' door daily?

Idea for Prayer

Pray for Ana as she seeks to share Christ with Albanians. Ask God to grant her an abundance of wisdom to meet the overwhelming needs of the people. Pray also that many zealous and committed young men and women will apply to the Resurrection of Christ Theological Academy to receive training like Ana's.

Lynette Holm Hoppe *(1989) and her husband Nathan have two children, Tristan and Katherine. She served in the Orthodox Church of Albania as well as the Orthodox Christian Mission Center (OCMC) from 1998 to 2006 when she passed into the presence of her Lord after her struggle with cancer ended. Her work included graphic design and instruction, homeschool, OCMC outreach/evangelism program, writing and editing and organizing creative projects for children and youth camps.*

BANGLADESH
When something seems impossible

. . . .

Little Nudgy Finds a Home

Beth Tebbe

Bangladesh is a country of curving rivers where beautiful sailboats glide through the waterways. The rivers Ganges (Padma), Meghna and Jamuna (Brahmaputra) wind their way through Bangladesh into the Bay of Bengal. While these rivers often bring devastating floods, the same floods replenish the soil and make possible the livelihood of the farmers.

Scripture – Exodus 2:5-10
Then Pharaoh's daughter…saw the basket among the reeds and sent her female slave to get it. She opened it and saw the baby. He was crying and she felt sorry for him. "This is one of the Hebrew babies," she said. Then his sister asked Pharaoh's daughter, "Shall I go and get one of the Hebrew women to nurse the baby for you?" "Yes, go," she answered. And the girl went and got the baby's mother. Pharaoh's daughter said to her, "Take this baby and nurse him for me, and I will pay you." So the woman took the baby and nursed him. When the child grew older, she took him to Pharaoh's daughter and he became her son. She named him Moses, saying, "I drew him out of the water."

Story
When my husband Jim served as pastor in Bangladesh, we had our services in the meeting hall of a Catholic girls' school. One Sunday Jim was asked to give an announcement by one of the Catholic sisters that a premature baby had been abandoned on the doorstep of the orphanage.

Although they tried to care for her, they just didn't have the resources. Was there an expatriate family who could take her and give her extra care and attention? After the service, since Jim was busy, I talked to the Catholic sister and became convinced this was something we should do.

Living in such a populated country at the time, we weren't planning on having any more children, but I thought that we would all profit from having a baby in the house. Well, fools step in where angels fear to tread! I pictured someone to cuddle, to help teach the boys to be gentle and to nurse along until she grew ready to be adopted. Little "Nudgy-Pudgy," as we nicknamed her, was a 28-week preemie, weighing about two pounds. In the United States today, the probability is high she could be easily saved; however, in Bangladesh the prognosis was not good.

Although Jim teases me that I went overseas to practice medicine without a license, I have no medical background. Nudgy couldn't tolerate the simplest formula from the local market. When she became seriously dehydrated we took her to the "Cholera Hospital" and had to beg for attention. The Catholic sister who had come with us baptized her. Finally we found a doctor willing to give her a saline injection to restore her fluid balance.

A wonderful nurse who had worked in refugee camps then taught us how to tube-feed her. We collected breast milk from many of the nursing mothers in the congregation (our refrigerator was full of numerous marked little bottles) and fed her around the clock every two hours. Each feeding included risk as it involved inserting the tube, which could have punctured her tiny esophagus (or worse, gone to her lungs had we used the wrong one). Hygiene, never easy in the tropics, had to be strict. We had no incubator, but Bangladesh fulfilled the incubator requirements with its temperature and humidity level in August.

Little Nudgy grew to more than five pounds and a lovely American family wanted to adopt her. Getting Nudgy out of the country became another huge answer to prayer as policy suddenly turned against international adoptions. God used the ambassador from Korea to advocate for us and when the family prepared to leave the country little Elizabeth Ann had her papers. The couple had given her my name.

Today I'm wise enough to be shocked at what we did, knowing as little as we did about proper care. But when resources run slim, we are all called to do things that would seem foolish in other circumstances. God gave us a marvelous example of the value he puts on a little baby whose fate seemed hopeless, but of infinite worth to him.

Journaling Topic

How would you have responded to Jim's announcement about Nudgy needing a home?

Idea for Prayer

Pray for orphans around the world and the agencies that work with international adoptions and foster care.

Beth Tebbe (1997) has served with InterServe in Pakistan, Bangladesh, Cyprus and the United States. Her ministry has included raising four children, teaching English as a foreign language, leading Bible studies, discipling women and providing hospitality for those around her. Currently, she and her husband Jim lead the InterVarsity Urbana Conference team in Madison, Wisconsin.

BOLIVIA
When facing opposition

. . . .

Women Facing
Opposition in Ministry

Francesca Crane

Although Bolivia is a landlocked nation, it does have access to the Atlantic Ocean via the Paraguay River. The eastern boundaries of its western plateau are covered by thick forests. In the west lies the world's largest salt flats, known as "the Salar de Uyuni." Aside from their land, Bolivians are also known for their *fiestas*—an important part of the Bolivian culture. The origin of a *fiesta* usually surrounds a religious or political event and includes folk music, dancing processions, food, drinking, ritual and sometimes unrestrained behavior.

Scripture – Galatians 3:28

There is neither Jew nor Greek, slave nor free, male nor female, for you are all one in Christ Jesus.

Story

While teaching on the topic of women in leadership at a Bolivian Christian conference, I received an invitation to speak to some women at another gathering. Both conferences were sponsored by two separate groups that work in Bolivia. Knowing that the other group held a conservative view of women in ministry, I felt hesitant about accepting their offer. However, since the request came directly from the organization's president of women's ministries, who had previously heard my views on the topic, I felt comfortable enough with speaking.

On a very hot, tropical day another missionary colleague of mine and I arrived at the camp where the conference would convene. As I taught throughout the day, I was surprised to find that the women participated enthusiastically. During the dinner break the president of the convention introduced me to the pastor who would preach at the evening worship service. He simply nodded in acknowledgement of my presence and walked away.

The president apologized for his behavior and hurried away to make arrangements for the service. My knowledge of Bolivia told me that the pastor's behavior seemed strange—greetings are very important in their culture. But I soon remembered that the pastor came from another South American country, which may have had different cultural norms.

The evening worship service began well until someone introduced the pastor. He stood and addressed the audience. Raising his Bible above his head, he started yelling at the women in rebuke. He told them that they had been listening to blasphemy. They had no place in ministry that put them in any kind of leadership over men. From his perspective, God prohibited women to preach or become pastors. He then proceeded through the Bible, giving examples of "women who knew their place." At the end of the sermon he turned, looked directly at me and said, "You must send this handmaiden of Satan away and never listen to her again!" I practically went into a state of shock. The pastor stomped out the door and left the campgrounds. He was scheduled to return the next evening for another service.

My colleague and I returned to my room where she asked me if the pastor had actually said what she thought she heard. I confirmed her doubts and we wrestled with what to do next. Should I continue to teach the next day? Should we leave at once? We didn't know what to do, so we prayed all night hoping God would give us a direct answer. In the morning the president apologized for what had happened and asked me to stay and teach the women. Believing this to be an answer to our prayers, I agreed.

The questions and conversations that followed my morning presentation, which focused on discovering spiritual gifts, were remarkable. Wanting to encourage the women more, I quickly trained several leaders so that we could break into small discussion groups. Within the groups, the women expressed openly their concerns about how to use their gifts more effectively in their local churches.

When the time for the evening worship service came, the pastor did not return. Instead a woman stood up to testify that she had not used her spiritual gifts to take the gospel to others because she feared being ostracized by her church community. As a result of what she learned from the conference, she told the crowd that she would use her gifts no matter what the consequences. Although she didn't know exactly how she was going to do it, she knew that with God's help everything would be worked out. She then proceeded to challenge the others to use their spiritual gifts to further the kingdom of God in their local churches and communities.

Reflecting upon this experience, I could not help but wonder what happened to the women when they returned to their local churches. I found myself praying for them regularly. It was not until some months later that I was dismayed to find out that the women's societies had been disbanded, and the women could no longer meet without a man present.

Despite this development, the women began to witness in their neighborhoods and communities. They started evangelistic groups and held meetings in their homes. Seizing the opportunity to use their gifts, God blessed their outreach. Dozens of men, women and children have come to faith, been baptized and attend local churches because of them. Although their struggle continues within the churches, these women have learned to use their gifts creatively and to minister wherever they find the opportunity.

Journaling Topic

When, where and how do women in ministry use God's gifts in the midst of opposition? Are there any alternatives? How do women experience and serve God appropriately in a male-dominated society?

Idea for Prayer

Pray that women will remain faithful and use their gifts in their communities.

Francesca Crane (2001) is married and has three children. She has served as a professor of missiology and director of the School of World Missions at a seminary in Bolivia. Since 2005 she has been executive director of Bridge of Hope in Pennsylvania.

BORNEO

When searching for someone

. . . .

A Trip Worth Making

Christy Reed

Considered part of Southeast Asia, Borneo ranks as the third largest island in the world, and is one of the 17,508 islands that make up the Malay Archipelago and Indonesia. The island divides politically between Indonesia, Malaysia and Brunei. The rainforests make up the only natural habitat for the endangered Bornean orangutan. The indigenous people continue to fight to preserve the environment against loggers and transmigrasi settlers—the name given to the massive migration of poor farmers.

Scripture – Luke 15:8-10

Or suppose a woman has ten silver coins and loses one. Does she not light a lamp, sweep the house and search carefully until she finds it? And when she finds it, she calls her friends and neighbors together and says, "Rejoice with me; I have found my lost coin." In the same way, I tell you, there is rejoicing in the presence of angels of God over one sinner who repents.

Story

I had planned on accompanying the public health team into a nearby village but the trip had been cancelled. I found the day unexpectedly free. I walked into the small rooming house known as the "motel" and wondered what to do with myself. Natalia's letter came to my mind…

and an idea started to form.

Natalia had been my first convert. When I was six my family moved from the hospital complex in Borneo where I'd grown up to the thriving metropolis of Bengkayang—about thirty minutes away. Compared to the jungled province of western Borneo, five thousand people and two streets made this the big city! My brother and I did not feel particularly pleased about the move since all our friends remained back in the hospital complex. When we complained to our parents, however, they explained to us that we needed to live in Bengkayang to tell the people there about Jesus. This seemed to be a noble enough task to my young mind, so I embarked with gusto on an evangelical campaign to win the local children to Christ. I figured if I did that, I could eventually go back to live with my friends at the hospital.

Thus grew my motivation to share Christ with Natalia, the niece of our next-door neighbor. I was seven and she was ten. I wish I could say my evangelism was culturally sensitive and well-grounded, but from what I remember this was hardly the case. I recall reiterating the horrors of the frightening place we called *Neraka* (hell) several times; with this I was able to coerce a prayer out of my friend. Although slightly less than an ideal start to our relationship, the Lord, who can use even insensitive 7-year-olds for his purposes, blessed our friendship and we became best friends.

This brings me back to my free day. I was now nineteen and returning to the island of my youth to work with a public health team for a summer. Over the years Natalia and I had continued correspondence, though fleeting. Just a couple of weeks before I had received a letter saying that she was married to a Hindu man named Nyoman, and working in a palm factory just inland from where I was staying. I decided to use my free day to go and visit her. Although I was idealistic (and inexperienced) about the fine art of traveling in Borneo, Rita, my friend and self-appointed caretaker, offered to go with me.

The "bus" was a small van painted in bright colors with chickens, luggage, produce and people crammed into (and hanging out of) every available space. I felt very excited, much to Rita's chagrin, to obtain the most well-ventilated spot on the bus. I hung out the side of the van, with both feet on the step that led up into the bus. I held onto an attached metal bar for dear life. With the wind blowing in my face as we traveled down the winding mountain road, I could feel the excitement of the journey well up inside me.

We reached Bengkayang where we found a slightly larger bus that would take us to the town closest to the plantation. After numerous stops, we rolled into the river town of Sanggau Ledo. Not knowing what else to do, we decided to walk down the only main street in town. Since we were the only foreigners to be seen for several hours in any direction, we attracted considerable attention. Dorcas, an old friend and a self-made businesswoman who operated a small store, welcomed us into her sparse living quarters. After Rita explained the reason for our journey, Dorcas obtained some *ojekan*—a service where young men with motorcycles take you somewhere for a fee. After determining a price, she hopped on one motorcycle; Rita and I hopped onto another.

We traveled in the heat, passing land stripped of its vegetation (palm oil farming depletes the soil of much of its nutrients). The sun beat down on us and the red dust blew as we traveled onward down the deserted road. Passing occasional shacks where curious dogs and children starred at us, I wondered if we would ever find Natalia. The sudden stop of the motorcycle abruptly jerked me out of my reverie. Dorcas arranged for our ride to wait for us, and we hopped off. After asking several people for help, one woman indicated that she knew who we were searching for. She led us through a small worker's village, built up on stilts, and stopped at a house. We climbed the wooden steps, calling for Natalia. And then…there she stood.

Her eyes scanned back and forth from Rita to Dorcas to me, and then she apologized for her casual state. Rita, who had known us both when we were children, asked about Natalia's job and husband; however, I felt tongue-tied. So I sat silently as she fed us instant noodles, and Rita carried on most of the conversation. Occasionally, Natalia would say something and look at me; in those moments, I knew the bond we shared still transcended culture, language, age, education, lifestyle and even time. But without warning, our different worlds would create another divide. She and I had our picture taken together in her office. After an hour or so, she had to get back to work, and Rita and I needed to make it back to the hospital before nightfall.

Before we left I shook Natalia's hand to say goodbye and asked if I could pray with her. She laughed nervously and said, "Oh, Christy, I can't pray anymore." In broken Indonesian, I attempted to explain God's love for her and his longing to hear her speak to him. After we prayed, Rita, Dorcas and I hopped onto the bikes behind our drivers and rode away.

I have not seen Natalia since. She wrote to tell me about the birth of her first child—a boy. Although time and distance continue to separate us, I will never forget the gift of that day when our covenant formed during childhood was renewed. Indeed, it was a trip worth making.

Journaling Topic

When was the last time you shared Christ with a friend? What was her/his response? What have you done recently to cultivate the relationship?

Idea for Prayer

Pray for Natalia and Nyoman. Pray for the people of Borneo that they might hear and receive the good news of Jesus Christ.

__Christy Reed__ (2003) works with the Mennonite Central Committee (MCC) in Indonesia where she teaches anthropology and English as a foreign language. She spent her formative years on various islands in the Indonesian Archipelago.

CHILE
When facing danger

. . . .

Shipwrecked

Shura Facanha

*I*slote Solitario, Beagle Channel, Chile
The southern coast of Chile resembles a labyrinth of man-made waterways, irregular peninsulas and scattered islands. One of these islands rests in the Beagle Channel off the coast of Chile. The name *Islote Solitario* appears on an Argentine government chart of the 1950s, and describes the island's position—*solitario* is a Spanish word meaning "solitary."

Scripture – Philippians 3:13b-14
But one thing I do: Forgetting what is behind and straining toward what is ahead, I press on toward the goal to win the prize for which God has called me heavenward in Christ Jesus.

Story
The engines stopped. The room turned suddenly black.

When the emergency lights came on, they cast an ominous yellow glow. The ship stood lifeless—still in the middle of the ocean—strong waves battering against its hull. I looked at my friend and muttered the only words that came to mind—"we're sunk."

On the cold, dark night of January 4, 1988, the M/V Logos set sail from Ushuaia, south of Argentina. The air hung heavy with the scent of the sea. When the big boat began to rock its hull in the ocean's waves, a storm broke loose—turning with the sea in a tumultuous dance.

My joining the ship crew only months ago came as something of a surprise. I knew God desired everything from me and I knew I wanted to serve him, but I had struggled with the specifics. Living on a floating home for the next two years of my life seemed a bit daunting. However, I wanted to learn humility and practice obedience so I joined the recruits of the M/V Logos.

The day I climbed the gangway remains fresh in my memory. Smells of fuel and oil perfumed the air on deck while crew members maintained the ship. That night as we sailed off the coast of Argentina, I stood on deck admiring the choppy waves—completely unaware of the tragedy we would face in the months ahead. I felt fully assured that my life and my future rested securely in the hands of God. Returning to bed, the loud hum of the generator rocked me to sleep like a seafarer's lullaby.

The day that followed is forever etched in my memory. After following the normal routine of departure, I made my way to the galley. My German friend Claudia and I planned to whip up a surprise birthday party. While we baked, we noticed that the sea seemed unusually rough—waves kept washing over the middle deck. Minutes before midnight the ship came to a sudden, abrupt stop. Plates and knives flew off the shelves and on top of us. I looked at my friend, who stood motionless, and took her hand. We did the only thing we knew we could do—we prayed.

I ran from the galley into my cabin to throw on an extra set of warm clothes and my lifejacket, as all the passengers gathered in the dining room, ready for instruction.

We learned that the ship had hit a cluster of submerged rocks known as Islote Solitario, located in the Beagle Channel off the coast of Chile. As the minutes passed we read the Bible aloud, seeking words of reassurance. Praying and singing, we waited upon the Lord. Suddenly God's presence filled the room. He hovered so sweet and so tender that we felt as though he were sitting right there in the midst of us. We felt covered by his love and surrounded with peace. In those moments, I felt prepared for anything he had in store—be it life or death.

Two hours after the ship had run aground I was nearly certain I was going to die. The ship had turned around, crushing the keel against the rock and leaving a gaping hole. I could see the water rushing in. We could hear the cracking of the ship against the rock. Chilean patrols had come to help, but the divers were sounding every fifteen minutes without success.

All efforts failed.

When the water started coming into the engine room, the captain knew the ship was lost. He gave the orders for evacuation—repeating those words that resound in my mind like a nightmare: "Abandon ship, abandon ship, abandon ship." It was 5:00 a.m.

The decks had become extremely slippery and the 30-degree list made evacuation seem almost impossible. With great difficulty, one by one we made our way to the lifeboats. As I climbed in, I found I was emotionally numb. Everyone sat quietly. No one panicked; no one cried.

We lost our personal belongings, but everyone on board was saved. The Chilean patrol rescued us from our lifeboats and took us to the island of Puerto Williams in the southernmost tip of South America.

Once on dry land I began to mull over the events that had just taken place and fear crept its way into my mind. Had I misinterpreted God's leading? His call on my life seemed to end so quickly. As I stood by some rocks covered with snow, on an island seemingly made of ice, Philippians 3:13b-14 came to my mind. "But one thing I do: Forgetting what is behind and straining toward what is ahead, I press on toward the goal to win the prize for which God has called me heavenward in Christ Jesus." Those words grabbed me, held me and hid me in Christ. The prize awaiting me in Jesus far outweighed the possessions I lost. I felt unexpectedly grateful for everything that had occurred: the calling, the shipwreck, the people—even the cold. It was nothing less than a privilege to have been on the M/V Logos when it went down—and even a greater honor to be allowed to live and tell the story.

That experience taught me that whatever circumstances of life we find ourselves in, whether we understand them or not, God is in control. He truly wants what is best for us. All we have to do is trust and obey. When I remember the day the Logos sank, I picture the old me being buried with the ship below the sea, and a new person rising. She now walks confidently with her Savior, who has rescued her in more ways than one.

Journaling Topic

What are some circumstances you are presently facing that need to be released to God?

Idea for Prayer

Pray for Christians today in our global community who may be facing situations which appear to be a "shipwreck." Pray that in every situation they can do all things through Christ who strengthens them (Phil. 4:11-13).

Shura Facanha (2000) has served with Operation Mobilization (OM) in Ecuador for more than fifteen years. She and her husband Roberto oversee OM's work in several Latin American countries. They have two children.

CHINA
When finances are limited

. . . .

The Christmas Violin

Ming

Ranking the third largest in land mass, China is the most populous country in the world. It is the home of the renowned "Great Wall of China"—spreading over four thousand miles—and is recognized for its long history and ancient traditional culture. Located along the coastline of southeast Asia, the land consists of a wide variety of terrain including the longest river in Asia, the Yangtze. China ranks as the world's top coal-producing country, abundant in minerals, animals and plants. Although admittedly an atheist nation, many still adhere to Confucianism, Buddhism and Taoism; Christianity, however, is growing underground.

Scripture – Matthew 2:11
On coming to the house, they saw the child with his mother Mary, and they bowed down and worshipped him. Then they opened their treasures and presented him with gifts of gold and of incense and of myrrh.

Story
Just before Christmas, when I wondered what to get for our children, an American friend told me about a local violinmaker. He created a beautiful violin for someone that Christmas, but the person changed his mind at the last minute and now the violin was for sale. My friend, a violinist himself, expressed to me that the man's work was excellent, and he recommended that I take a look at the violin.

I still remember the time we went to see it. On that cold night, we had voyaged to another part of the city to find the violinmaker. His apartment sat tucked away on the third floor of an old building. His home looked simple and bare, but he expressed delight in our interest in buying his violin. He carefully covered his tattered sofa with an old blanket and offered us a seat.

After he left the room, we heard him moving some things around in his bedroom. A few minutes later he emerged with a beautiful violin case which he carefully opened to reveal his masterpiece. With great delicacy, he took the beloved instrument out and explained how it had been made. After what seemed like a long time I inquired about the cost of the violin. I knew it would be expensive, but I also knew that if I bought a violin in America, it would have cost much more.

When we returned home we realized that we didn't have enough money for the violin, so my husband and I prayed that the Lord would provide the funds. I knew that under different circumstances we could have easily bought our son a violin. Had we stayed in America, we could have given our son an even more expensive one but because we chose another path, we were limited; I felt terrible. Within a few days we got word that someone else wanted to buy the violin, but we would be given an opportunity to purchase it first. I didn't know what to do, but I knew that God would make a way so I said yes.

At the beginning of that semester I had agreed to have my salary from my teaching position withheld in order to help the school through a tight semester. In December the situation greatly improved and within a few days the office offered to give me my salary for the semester. The amount I received slightly topped the cost of the violin. I could hardly believe it—the timing couldn't have been better. I bought the violin and gave it to our son as a Christmas gift. He loved it, and on Christmas morning he played for us. God had provided the funds for that violin in an unexpected way that blessed us all. We saw firsthand how God provides for his children.

Although I have often lamented over the things we couldn't give our children because we chose to serve overseas, over and over again God has shown me that in our obedience we gave our children far greater gifts than any we could have bought. Our children's experiences have enriched them in ways far more precious than any other gifts. I know this now, and take great delight in God's design.

Journaling Topic

When have you faced limited finances? How did you see God provide?

Idea for Prayer

Pray for the financial needs of cross-cultural workers.

Ming (2003) (a pseudonym) works as a professional in this location. She loves the people and is committed to gaining their trust and respect so she might earn a hearing for the gospel in their nation.

EAST AFRICA
When turning evil to good

. . . .

A God Who Uses the Broken

Anne

A beautiful region which touches the Indian Ocean, East Africa's borders are loaded with the history and culture of its diverse population. Perhaps known best for its spectacular wildlife, a number of interesting phenomena attract tourists from all over the world. In addition, the Great Rift Valley spans this region where some of the earliest evidence of humanity has been discovered.

Scripture – 2 Corinthians 1:3-5

Praise be to the God and Father of our Lord Jesus Christ, the Father of compassion and the God of all comfort, who comforts us in all our troubles, so that we can comfort those in any trouble with the comfort we ourselves have received from God. For just as the sufferings of Christ flow over into our lives, so also through Christ our comfort overflows.

Story

During my three years in Africa I fell in love with God's creation. From the beautiful landscapes of the breathtaking beaches to the summit of familiar mountains, I loved the land. I loved the culture, from the rural villages to the urban cities. I loved the work of teaching in a Bible club at a girl's high school, as well as teaching the Bible to street boys at various outreach centers. I especially loved the African people as I came to know them, work with them and develop friendships.

Over time, one of these friendships blossomed into something more. I was not looking for a romantic relationship, but one developed. After a year of friendship and dating, as well as a four-month engagement, I found myself married into the African culture. We thought that we had read and prepared for our cross-cultural marriage, but there was one vital topic our books failed to mention—domestic violence.

Shortly after the wedding, my husband began to physically abuse me. I had dreamt of a "perfect" marriage, of having a constant partner to share life and ministry with, but my dream turned into a nightmare. I felt devastated. I knew that what was happening was not right. I knew that I did not have to endure the abuse, but because of embarrassment and stubbornness I remained in the marriage. My only hope was that God would hear my prayers and make things right. At first, I tried to get my husband to seek help. I tried to get him to go to counseling with me. Others came in to confront him, but nothing worked. I hated divorce and fought against it, but at the same time, I knew that I was moving toward it. What else could I do? My marriage was over and the way I was living was not what God intended for me. I knew the time had come to get out.

By that time, my husband and I had been in the States for about a year and a half. We had left Africa to pursue further education with the intent of returning once we finished our degrees. Since he was already taking classes at a school in California where we lived, I returned home to Chicago during the divorce process. During this time I became impassioned about women's issues. I couldn't stand watching television programs that showed women being taken advantage of or being abused. I was appalled at the lack of biblical materials addressing the issue of domestic violence, emotional mistreatment and abuse of women in general. I began to wonder what I was going to do for God as a 28-year old, divorced ex-missionary? I was a Christian! This wasn't supposed to happen. What kind of a witness was I? Who would listen to me in the future? I was scarred. Could God still use me for his glory?

It was a slow process, but God showed me that he still had a plan for my future. He still wanted to use me—he had just narrowed the focus to a specific area. I would now use my firsthand experience with domestic violence to help women in similar situations. Upon recognition of this passion I decided the time had finally arrived to further my education. I had wanted to pursue a Masters in Community Development upon returning to the States, but due to my location after the divorce, I decided to pursue a Masters in Intercultural Studies from Wheaton College instead.

During my studies I was able to build on my experiences of living and working in a cross-cultural setting. I researched various issues related to the empowerment of women with regard to their original role as God intended for them. I also studied in depth the various issues of violence women face. I looked at Scripture to see how the Word addresses such issues, so I could build a biblical stance for the empowerment of women. How God will use me now that my degree is finished, I do not know. I do know he is a God who can take evil and turn it into good. He is a God who comforts us so that we can learn to comfort others. And I know he will use me to comfort women around the world so that they may know him as I do.

Journaling Topic

How has God taken a difficult circumstance in your life and used it for his glory?

Idea for Prayer

Pray for the women of the world who are suffering under the oppression of social injustices.

Anne (2005) (a pseudonym) served as a missionary in a region of Africa working primarily with street children. With an MA in Intercultural Studies, she has a heart to pursue work in the field of advocacy as it relates to social injustices faced by women.

EASTERN EUROPE

When traditions open up opportunities

. . . .

A Lesson from a
Muslim Holiday Tradition

Clara

The definition of Eastern Europe constantly changes. Vaguely defined, it's an area from Russia to Central Europe on the eastern part of the continent. Although it is sometimes utilized to identify the countries in Europe that were under Communist regimes, the boundaries of the term change depending on the context. From idyllic lakes and stately castles to small towns steeped in tradition, Eastern Europe is both antiquated and beautiful. Perhaps only its inhabitants have created more beauty, with such notable individuals as Mozart, Andy Warhol and missionaries Methodius and Cyril indigenous to the land.

Scripture – I John 2:2
He is the atoning sacrifice for our sins, and not only for ours but also for the sins of the whole world.

Story
While serving in this country as a cross-cultural worker I had the privilege of living in a house with a Muslim family. They offered me my own apartment while they lived in the rest of the house. Our relationship grew so quickly that we eventually considered each other as adopted family. Living in such close proximity to them gave me opportunities to demonstrate a Christ-like lifestyle in both word and deed.

They asked questions about my "religion," and we discussed the differences between my beliefs and theirs. Although they saw my life and the lives of my Christian friends, they still clung tightly to their religion.

One day as I observed the family perform a ritual for one of their Muslim holidays, the reality of the spiritual struggle and the differences between our religions especially impacted me. This particular holiday comes the month after Bajram (the feasting celebration after the lengthy fasting of Ramadan). Traditionally, families slaughter a sheep (or two or more, or a cow, depending on their amount of wealth) and give part of the meat to the poor. I had observed this tradition before from a distance, but it didn't affect me until I saw a sheep slain right outside my apartment window. The unfortunate animal had been brought to the house the day before, and ran around the yard until that morning—the "appointed time."

The men of the extended family performed the following ritual: First, they slit the sheep's throat and drained the blood onto the ground. Then they hung the carcass on a tree by its back legs, and began to cut up the body—in time, they even brought it to the sidewalk and chopped it with an axe—splashing blood onto my door.

As I watched this ritual from my apartment (trying not to be conspicuous), the reality of the Old Testament sacrifices came to life. So this is what some of the process may have looked like for the Israelites, when they tried to take care of their sins, I thought. As I pondered this, a spiritual exuberance came over me: This is why Jesus came! He came to give his life as the final sacrifice to forever take care of our sin problem.

Although I continued to stand there and watch, I felt like dancing around my house. The biblical truth of Christ's atonement really impacted me; however, my joy was coupled with an intense sadness. These people I loved still did not understand who Jesus is and that he came as the perfect sacrificial lamb for their sins. They remained blinded by religion. They needed to do enough good things so that, hopefully, they might make it to Paradise. The thought renewed my commitment to pray for them, live a faithful witness and take advantage of opportunities that the Lord would give to relate his good news with them. Soon they called me up to the big holiday feast. I went with an increased passion to show them the awe-inspiring perfect sacrifice of Jesus.

Journaling Topic

What opportunities have you taken to discuss traditions and spiritual issues with people from other religious traditions?

Idea for Prayer

Pray for workers like Clara who minister in sensitive areas of the world in order to bring the gospel of Jesus Christ to Muslims.

Clara *(2004) (a pseudonym) serves as a professional in an undisclosed location. She loves the people and understands the long-term commitment required to build trust and respect. Her perseverance has earned her a hearing for the gospel in this context.*

ECUADOR
When facing disappointment

. . . .

Hindsight is 20/20

Youngchu Song

Although Ecuador ranks as the smallest country in the rugged Andean highlands, it encompasses an array of indigenous cultures, well-preserved colonial architecture, volcanic landscapes and dense rain forests. When in Quito, you are never more than a day's drive from a trek through the Amazonian jungle, a snow-swept ascent on an active volcano, a friendly haggle with indigenous *artesanos* or a swim on a tropical beach.

Scripture – Isaiah 55:8-9
"For my thoughts are not your thoughts, neither are your ways my ways,"
declares the Lord. "As the heavens are higher than the earth, so are my
ways higher than your ways, and my thoughts than your thoughts."

Story
With much excitement and anticipation, I arrived in Ecuador to serve at a large Covenant school. The first evangelical Christian high school built in Quito, it has long since served the poor. My role called for strengthening the English language department by providing training for the teachers and resources for the students. Little did I know that for the first two years all I would see would be overcrowded classrooms led by teachers who received little pay and support for their efforts. I also had to deal with my own experiences of personal failure, unfulfilled projects and witnessing unfair practices. To say the least, I became disappointed

and discouraged.

Yet in the midst of these discouraging times, God gave me special relationships with the Ecuadorian teachers. Their invitations into their homes for meals greatly encouraged me. They constantly gifted me with creative cards and expressed their gratitude for my presence at the school. Although I sometimes doubted my calling to Ecuador, God used these teachers to reassure me that he was doing something special in my life and in the lives of my new friends.

Just as I neared the end of my second year of teaching (as well as the fulfillment of my plans to return to the States and teach in a public school), I was offered a position at an international missionary (MK) school in Quito and took it as God's leading to stay in the country. Although the school is run by North Americans, one of its special features is the large growing population of Asian students (mostly Korean and Chinese) to whom I teach Korean history and culture, as well as English as a second language (ESL). It provides a unique opportunity to serve such a broad array of students in one location—Latin Americans, Asians and North Americans. As a Korean American living in Ecuador, I have seen the advantages of being bicultural. Not only have I been able to promote intercultural understanding among students of various ethnic backgrounds, but less culture shock occurs because of the commonalities between Latin and Asian cultures.

I have come to realize that hindsight is always twenty-twenty. Even though my first few years proved difficult, I remain thankful for the time I had in the Ecuadorian school system. My experiences taught me a lot about the culture, language and high value placed on relationships, as well as how to depend on the Lord when experiencing disappointment. If I had started my time at the MK school, I would not have had the opportunity or time to develop close friendships with the Ecuadorian teachers. The Lord's thoughts and ways are not always mine.

As I look toward the future, I am renewed, refreshed and excited to see how God will continue to use the experiences and gifts he has placed in my life in order to help me grow and learn in Ecuador. Having experienced his faithfulness in my own ups and downs as a Christian educator, I know that I am better equipped to teach these international children about culture, language and the One who created them for his glory.

Journaling Topic

Think about some disappointment that you have faced. How did you handle it? What did you learn about God? What did you learn about yourself?

Idea for Prayer

Pray for the encouragement of school administrators, teachers and other personnel who work with missionary children and their families from different cultures.

Yongchu Song (2002) serves as a teacher of missionary children in Quito, Ecuador with the Evangelical Covenant Church, known as Inglesia del Pacto Evangélico, where she is involved in teacher training, classroom instruction and curriculum development. Yongchu loves interacting with a wide range of international students, influencing both their spiritual and academic development.

FIJI ISLANDS

When the cost is extreme

. . . .

Counting the Cost

Becky DeBerry Bryant

Recognized as the focal point of the Pacific, Fiji lies just east of Australia. According to legend, chief Lutunasobasoba led his people from Southeast Asia to the land of Fiji, where the Melanesians and Polynesians mixed to develop a highly creative society. Today Fiji plays a major role in regional affairs. The Fijian culture is intricate, and their traditions are rich. One craft that Fijians have practiced for generations is *tapa* making. *Tapa*, a rough cloth made from the pounded bark of the mulberry, is decorated and used for ceremonial clothing and house decorations.

Scripture – Psalm 37:1-5, 7

Do not fret because of evil men…Trust in the Lord and do good; dwell in the land…Delight yourself in the Lord and he will give you the desires of your heart. Commit your way to the Lord; trust in him and he will do this…Be still before the Lord and wait patiently for him.

Story

While serving my first term in Gabon, Africa, a co-worker challenged me to consider continuing to faithfully serve God cross-culturally. Would I remain a missionary when it no longer seemed convenient, comfortable or the cost too extreme? In more than twenty years of overseas service, as both a single and married missionary with Child Evangelism Fellowship (CEF), I have had plenty of time to ponder and respond to that challenge.

After eight years in Gabon, I married Kent, a CEF missionary based in the Fiji Islands. We felt excited about combining our skills and spiritual gifts to continue to train nationals to reach children for Christ. However, it did not take me long to realize that "Fiji time" is just as inconvenient as "Gabonese time." More specifically, a promised six-week processing time stretched into six months of waiting for our work permit renewal. The adoption of our Fiji-born Indian daughter took ten months to complete. A minor "fender bender" took six months to repair (the paint job had to be redone four times over the span of a year). My frustrations continued to mount. Delays continued to accumulate. I clung to the actions exhorted in Psalm 37:1-5: Fret not, trust, delight, commit, rest and wait patiently.

Besides getting used to "Fiji time," we were further dismayed by an unexpected event that occurred when my parents arrived for a much-anticipated visit. Within twenty-four hours of their arrival we became embroiled in a political crisis. Seven armed men stormed the Fiji Parliament building, taking the Indian Prime Minister and many others as hostages. We watched the news in horror as a number of Fijians began to loot and burn Indian-owned businesses in the capital city.

A dusk-to-dawn curfew was imposed and armed soldiers erected check points throughout the island. The nights filled with bloodshed and death and I felt overwhelmed with fear. The situation seemed only to grow more chaotic. Economic sanctions were imposed, meaning supermarket shelves sat empty. The American Embassy issued a warning for all Americans to leave Fiji immediately, but we couldn't. We had not yet fulfilled all requirements for a permanent US visa for our adopted daughter. We had no choice but to remain. I found myself continually repeating my son's memory verse, "When I am afraid, I will trust in you" (Ps. 56:3).

The coup made life very uncomfortable. Some villagers decided to follow the example of the coup leaders and seized the hydro-electric dam. As a result, we had unpredictable power and water cuts. Either I didn't have water to cook and to wash, or we had no power for the fans, office equipment and household appliances. I responded with anger. Once again, God used Psalm 37 to offer me clear actions I could take to trust him: Cease from anger. I remembered something Warren Wiersbe once said: God does not expect us to be comfortable, but to be conformable. Was God asking me to be conformed to Jesus Christ when our water and power were cut off? When political unrest haunted our doorstep? When our baby daughter's safety might be at risk? This seemed to be an impossible expectation.

Our family suffered from the coup-related stress, and our stateside families remained anxious about our safety. For the first time I began to feel it might be too costly to remain—but we did. Our insistence on integrity cost us dearly—we lost a friendship with another missionary family, as well as a "church home" in Fiji. We were overcome with a "weariness of the soul," but just as we were ready to give up things began to stabilize politically. After we received our papers for our daughter we meditated on several passages—including Psalm 37 and Hebrews 12:1–3. Our focus changed from the inconvenience, discomfort and personal cost of ministry to the Lord Jesus Christ and the cost he paid to become our Savior. Our commitment was to the One who loves the people of Fiji infinitely more than we can imagine, and to obey his call upon our lives.

Journaling Topic

How do you respond when the cost of ministry seems extreme?

Idea for Prayer

Pray for minority groups who face persecution worldwide. Pray for peace, interracial respect and justice. Pray for the safety of workers in volatile areas of the world.

Becky DeBerry Bryant (1992) serves with Child Evangelism Fellowship (CEF) in Fiji. With her husband Kent and two children she trains nationals to reach children for Christ. She worked as a single missionary in Gabon, Africa with CEF for eight years.

HUNGARY

When searching for truth

. . . .

Released from Captivity

Melody Scott

Divided into three sections by the rivers Danube and Tisza, Hungary is a landlocked nation, strategically placed between Western Europe and the Balkan Peninsula. Hungary has become known for its beautiful lakes, hot springs and classical music. Although the World Wars have turned millions of ethnic Hungarians into refugees, on two significant occasions Hungary has opened up its own borders to refugees. The first opened to those escaping communism, and the second to those fleeing the conflict in Kosovo. Today the United Nations has succeeded in resettling the majority of displaced individuals, but many still live in the communal camps of surrounding countries where they are cared for by international relief agencies.

Scripture—Jeremiah 29:10-14

> *"The truth is that you will be in Babylon for...years. But then I will come and do for you all the good things I have promised, and I will bring you home again. For I know the plans I have for you," says the Lord. "They are plans for good and not for harm, to give you a future and hope. In those days when you pray, I will listen. If you look for me in earnest, you will find me when you seek me. I will be found by you," says the Lord. "I will end your captivity and bring you home again to your own land."'*

Story

The air hovered thick with the disheartening heaviness of despair, but there remained a shadow of celebration on the faces of the children as we entered the gates of this place. This was home to approximately four hundred people from different nations: Serbs and Muslims evading the Kosovo conflict, Afghans fleeing the Taliban, Africans escaping war and the AIDS crisis in their homeland and many others who vacated their country for a variety of reasons.

This was a refugee camp and the people here lived within a system similar to a homeless shelter: families received one dormitory room, limited food and clothing, $15/month and then were seemingly forgotten. Hundreds shared one small bathroom facility, a tiny kitchenette and a lone TV located in a large room with four wooden benches. Indeed, everyone there had come from desperate circumstances.

Numerous children were born and raised in the camp. Although they had the right to attend a local school, many chose not to go because of the language barriers. Many of these little ones suffered silently from abuse due to the dire circumstances of their family. Rage was not uncommon among children in the camp. This place was a prison. For me and those I had come to work with, this place was an opportunity for anyone who could offer its inhabitants a glimpse of what it means to have a hope and a future. I found people earnestly searching for spiritual and emotional freedom in spite of their physical captivity.

It was important, however, that spiritual matters be treated with sensitivity and caution. Many there had fled from political-religious wars, and many continued fighting within the camp over the same issues. Physical fights flared up regularly. However, one area that several ethnicities had in common was that they considered their dreams with serious contemplation. This became a point of prayer for those of us working in the camp— that God would speak to people through their dreams.

The resident missionary, a multi-lingual refugee and I attempted to start teaching English as an outlet for some of the children. Susannah, an 11-year-old refugee girl with long black hair and stunning eyes, would come to the room each day, search the bookshelf and secretly read the Bible before class. She begged us not to tell her family that she was reading Christian scriptures, for fear of their punishment. We promised and believed that it was only a matter of time before she discovered the truth about Jesus. Daily, we began to pray for her future and her earnest search.

Within weeks, we received an invitation to her family's room. Somewhat nervously, we entered—only to find ourselves being greeted with tiny, steaming glasses of Turkish coffee. Susannah, her baby brother and her stepmother were present. The stepmother disclosed the reason for our invitation: "I had a dream that three men with beards and long robes came and wanted Susannah to be baptized. I do not know what this means. Can you explain it?" In awe and near unbelief, the missionary and I exchanged glances with one another. My friend then delicately began to make clear the symbolism of baptism. Through her explanation she shared the good news of Jesus with this family.

Just after my friend offered to teach Susannah about Christ, her father burst into the room. "Susannah can choose whatever religion she wants," he said, "but I will not permit her to become a Christian." With those words he departed, and the stepmother whispered, "Just forget about what I asked." Our conversation changed, and we never revisited the topic.

A few months later Susannah and her family disappeared in the middle of the night. We believe that one of the local mafia groups arranged their escape from the camp. To this day I continue to pray for Susannah—wherever she may be. From our first meeting with her, my missionary friend and I trusted that the Lord would bring her to spiritual freedom. Now we pray for her family as well—that the Lord will continue to visit and speak to them through their dreams—ever drawing them toward salvation.

Journaling Topic

Has the Lord ever spoken to you through a dream? Consider Genesis 37:1-20, Daniel 2 or Acts 2:17.

Idea for Prayer

The current statistic from the United Nations is that roughly fifteen million people are displaced in refugee camps around the world. Pray for those who are displaced. Also, pray for the workers, that they will not grow weary in reflecting God's offer of a future and hope.

***Melody Scott** (2005) holds a BA in Christian Ministries and an MA in Intercultural Studies and Missions. She served with the Evangelical Friends Church for eight years. During this time, she volunteered for a short-term assignment to a refugee camp in Hungary, following the Kosovo crisis of the late 1990s. Her denomination assisted a church, which ministered in a private (vs. U.N.-based) refugee camp in a particular region. Melody works as a college instructor and freelance editor, specializing in intercultural communications. She serves at a not-for-profit organization, WorldView International in Cleveland, Ohio.*

INDIA
When you sense failure

. . . .

Flowers in a Wall

Sheri Lazarus

In ancient India a social system developed in which people were divided into separate close communities known as castes. The origin of the caste system is found in the Hindu religion; however, it affected the whole Indian society. The caste system in its religious form represents basically a division of society into four castes. The castes are arranged in a hierarchy and below them are the outcast. Practicing untouchability or discriminating against a person based on his/her caste is legally forbidden. The Indians have become more flexible in their caste system customs. In general the urban people in India are less strict about the caste system than the rural people. In cities people from different castes often mingle with each other, while in some rural areas discrimination is still based on castes.

Scripture – Matthew 19:26
Jesus looked at them and said, "With man this is impossible, but with God all things are possible."

Story
When I first moved to India I wondered what God had in mind. In a male-dominated, status-oriented society, I didn't know if anyone would even listen to a young, unmarried woman. Like most newcomers, I began to study the language, dreaming of the day when I could share my

faith in Hindi.

One day I struck up a conversation with an elderly Hindu "Auntie" at the home of some friends. On hearing that I was a Christian, Auntie proudly began to tell me how open-minded she was.

"All religions are the same," she said with conviction. "I sometimes worship in churches just like you. When I see a crucifix, I not only see Jesus, but also Krishna and Buddha and all the others. All gods, all religions, are the same!"

As I listened I grew more and more sad and uncomfortable; I wanted to share with her why I believe the Christian God is unique, but I had two major problems. First, in Indian culture, it is considered rude to disagree with elders. If I jumped in too fast, I ran the risk of alienating this Auntie, sabotaging our new relationship.

Second, Auntie didn't speak a word of English. I would have to share in Hindi, and my faltering language skills hardly seemed up to the challenge of a rigorous debate on religious philosophy.

Yet I knew I had to say something, so I began as respectfully as I knew how. Auntie listened politely, but I soon got the sense that something was not quite right. More conversation confirmed it. The Christian vocabulary that I had learned in language school and church did not mean a thing to her. Growing up Hindu, she had never heard words like "sin" and "grace" before and she was missing my point entirely. I was using Hindi, but we were not speaking the same language.

I tried using stories to explain, yet after each one Auntie would respond with a comment that reflected complete misunderstanding. Everything filtered through her own cultural and religious lens. I felt powerless.

We finished our conversation over an hour later. As Auntie stood to leave, she smiled, patted me on the head and said, "You are just a child. You don't know anything."

Completely dejected, I went home and cried. I felt like a complete failure. After all my training and study, I still could not communicate. Why couldn't I make her understand?

Through my tears, I prayed, "God, why did you bring me here? What use am I? I can't even share about you with one old lady. Tonight I felt like I was talking to a brick wall and expecting flowers to grow!"

Immediately, a picture came to me: Moses and all Israel were in front of a large rock and God was telling Moses to speak to the rock and water would flow out (Num. 20:7-8). Underneath the picture in my mind ran a caption: "With God all things are possible."

With that one image the Lord brought me comfort. What must Moses have thought when God told him to talk to a rock in order to get water? It must have sounded impossible.

Once before, Moses had struck a rock to get water. At least striking is action; he was doing something. But talking to a rock? It's ridiculous. In the end, Moses did not trust God enough to do a ridiculous thing. Relying on his own experience, he struck the rock instead. The water did come, but so did terrible consequences.

This was God's answer to me: "So what if you are trying to do the impossible? You are being obedient to me. If I tell you to talk to a wall, do it, and trust me to bring the 'flowers.' With me, all things are possible."

Often in my pride, I labor under the delusion that my ministry will be successful if I just work hard enough, using the right strategies and techniques. While those things are important, they will never be enough. Whatever our method, only the Lord can bring the fruit (or water from a rock, flowers from a brick wall and salvation in a hard heart.)

Journaling Topic

Write about a time when you relied more on your strategies and techniques than on God's provision. What did you learn from that situation?

Idea for Prayer

Pray for those people who consider themselves so "open-minded" that they consider all religions to be okay. Pray for the workers trying to reach these people.

Sheri Lazarus *(1998) has served in India for more than five years, most recently working with Engineering Ministries International (EMI). Her work has included cross-cultural training, teaching English as a foreign language, writing for publications, discipleship and development work.*

INDONESIA

When facing painful memories

. . . .

Reflections from a Copra Boat

Cara Hurley

The nation of Indonesia consists of islands surrounding the equator between the Indian and the Pacific Oceans. The total area of the archipelago measures nearly three times the size of Texas. Although it is made up of 17,508 islands, only six thousand are inhabited. One form of inter-island travel common to this area is the copra boat, a craft featured in this story.

Scripture – Psalm 119:75-76

I know, O Lord, that your laws are righteous, and in faithfulness you have afflicted me. May your unfailing love be my comfort, according to your promise to your servant.

Story

My stomach still clenches with panic every time I hear a strong gust of wind moving through the trees. The sound makes the memories of the small wooden copra boats rush back into my mind; this is then followed by the unusual scent of smoked coconut flesh and gasoline. Boat trips to the village became the terror of my life from the age of nine through eleven.

Our boat was nothing to be terrified of—at least three of four outboard motors propelled it from the stern. There was always cargo strapped to the roof, where agile crew members or passengers sometimes lounged. Inside, over the cargo below, a platform ran the length and breadth of the boat. There were no life jackets, except for those belonging to my family, and many times the windows were too small for the human body to crawl through. I always saw them there more for vomiting purposes than anything else. Had one of these boats gone down, we, along with all the others crammed into the small interior, would have been trapped.

Each boat trip lasted from nine to twelve hours, and many of them occurred at night when the sea was calmer. As time went by I began staying up all night during the journey, trying to quell my terror by singing and praying to Jesus. Sometimes the sea lay smooth as glass, but other times I watched lightning strike the water as I sang. We always had three or four months of normal life between boat trips, but even then I had nightmares—not to mention the panic that came whenever I heard a wind that reminded me of an ocean storm.

Boat trips aside, I loved the village life. At age eleven, I wrote in my journal, "Why couldn't every kid live like this?" I knew even then how immensely privileged I was, and I filled my journal with maps, detailed descriptions of games my Tabaru friends taught me and accounts of hikes to rice gardens hidden deep in the forest.

However, it was not the people, or even the boat trips that precipitated my deepest disappointment with God; it was malaria. The first attack was nearly fatal, but God spared my life. When my health stabilized, my parents decided the time had come to leave the village for a few months of rest and refreshment. The night before the boat trip, we prayed together for a calm ocean. For me, this represented an experiment in faith. I had a desperate desire for God to answer this prayer for a calm trip. But, alas, it was not to be. Sometime after this stormy, disappointing voyage ended my parents consented to let me go to boarding school; thus I left village life and the dreaded boat trips behind.

After I was married and attending graduate school, God brought my mind back to the bitter disappointment of that final boat trip. I had never doubted that he was able to calm the sea, but he simply didn't. To my childish eyes, God seemed capricious. As I wrote my reflections of the trip in my journal, I wept. I had never before comprehended how deep that childhood wound went, nor how it continued to affect my views of God.

But God's gentle hand soothed me. His light broke through, and I became able to write, "Behind it all, I need to realize that it was really, truly for GOOD...God used it in my life...God IS planning good for me." That day I understood more deeply that no matter how things look, God's intentions toward me are good. In this way God used a bitter memory and my disappointment with him to remind me of his goodness. Psalm 119:75 says, "In faithfulness you have afflicted me." Although I cannot always see how good is possible from difficult situations, I know that God sees farther than I can, and he invites me to rest in his unfailing love and goodness no matter where I am—even in a copra boat.

Journaling Topic

What past memories need healing in your life? What have you learned about God's character from these memories?

Idea for Prayer

Pray for missionary kids who experience many transitions in their lives. Pray for adjustment, friendships, schooling, health and other issues that God brings to mind.

Cara Hurley *(2004) grew up as a missionary kid in Indonesia. At age nine she moved with her parents on an assignment with Wycliffe Bible Translators to a remote village. Today she is married to Brian and teaches English as a second language to adult refugees in a community-based program. There she advocates for the people's needs as they resettle in the United States.*

JAPAN

When patience is required

. . . .

Cultivating the Gift of Patient Enduring

Holly Ann Bell

Surrounded by the waters of the Pacific, Japan is an East Asian cluster of more than three thousand islands. It is known as the "Land of the Rising Sun" and remains one of the world's leading industrialized countries. Because the land's mountainous regions are filled with both dormant and active volcanoes making it prone to earthquakes, many of its inhabitants safely crowd into a few cities along the coast. The population, primarily Japanese with some Korean and Chinese immigrants, is steeped in culture and highly respectful of its nation's traditional ways.

Scripture – Jeremiah 17:7-8

But blessed is the man who trusts in the Lord, whose confidence is in him. He will be like a tree planted by the water that sends out its roots by the stream. It does not fear when heat comes; its leaves are always green. It has no worries in a year of drought and never fails to bear fruit.

Story

The year 2000 started out with excitement and promise. We were in the process of purchasing the English conversation schools that we had been teaching and managing. We had two adorable children, the first American-Canadian children born in this hospital. Pat's (my husband) cousin was joining our teaching staff and we had a young couple from his home church in Canada who had been teaching for a year. Our little team busily reached out to the spiritually dark city of Hagi. We had learned the term "church saturation planting," but the Buddhists had already achieved that with a ratio of one temple per one hundred people. Hagi had two Protestant churches and one Catholic church. When we all got together for the annual prayer day, around seventy-five assembled; most were over the age of sixty. But we had rejoiced when Dr. Ichihara gave his life to Christ, and we felt thrilled and full of anticipation at what the Lord was doing.

Pat and I arrived in Hagi City in 1995 as young, fresh, excited idealists ready to share our faith, hope and love with the people the Lord brought into our lives. We had no idea what we were doing. Pat's focus had been Muslim studies, and we thought we were headed to a different land and culture. But with outstanding college debts, we received advice to pay off our debt and then come back to the mission. So we applied for teaching jobs in several countries.

Two positions became available in a small conversation school in Hagi. After much prayer, we accepted teaching jobs with a small secular school, thinking we would work for a year or two, then go to the Middle East. When Pat's great aunt heard the name Hagi, she remembered some distant relatives had started a church right after WW II in Hagi. We felt this was a strong confirmation that we were to head to Hagi. When we arrived we visited the church, but no one spoke English. However, we eventually ended up joining this little church and encouraging the sparse, geriatric congregation.

One year in Hagi turned into two and then three, and we kept extending our time, becoming more and more embedded into the life of this beautiful city. Then the opportunity came to buy the schools where we taught and managed. The church elder became excited about helping us out financially and pulled together two other men to contribute. Everyone seemed thrilled.

Then slowly, month by month, the realities and expectations of what that meant started to unfold. The obligation, the cultural implications, the continual miscommunication due to language and interpretation and the business styles became increasingly difficult and miserable. We embarrassed these men by not doing things their way. They didn't understand our goals and purposes. Relationships at church and among the school staff became strained.

We prayed and sought the Lord and requested prayer and wisdom from those who knew us well. We finally took a vacation back to the States for a month to get perspective. We looked back over the past five years where we had invested so heavily in relationships. The monthly music outreach was growing. Bible studies were springing up in Japanese homes by our teachers, people were being loved and prayed for. Students were hearing about Jesus. We realized this battle was more than a cultural business misunderstanding; we were fighting a spiritual battle.

So we stayed. We continually prayed and fasted for those who didn't understand us and we told the Lord if he wanted us to stay here, then he would need to provide the financing to buy out these men and gain control. Within a short period money came from several sources and in December 2000 we legally bought out the rights and territory of the Bell English Conversation School.

In 2001 we rejoiced to see our precious secretary Asami become a Christian. On the day of her baptism another young friend gave her heart to Jesus. The next year several more came to faith and we have seen more and more young people coming to the Lord.

The Lord is good and faithful. Over time, and with much prayer, the men who experienced so much frustration with us have come to forgive us, and we have forgiven them. We still worship in that church which now has a new young generation of people who love the Lord.

Our children attend local schools. Throughout the years our staff has been asked to teach English in every elementary and junior high school in Hagi, as well as several kindergartens and day care centers. I had the privilege of teaching English and culture on the local TV station. We started a Mother's Club, an outreach to young mothers for support and encouragement.

Pat has had many opportunities to share his faith through music, song, speaking and writing. He is also a wedding pastor and encourages new couples to allow Jesus into their marriage.

Each teacher has made an eternal impact here, not only through teaching but through a choral group, art shows, drama ministry and Bible studies. We never dreamed how much we would be humbled and tested, how much we would learn from the people we came to serve or that we would still be in Hagi ten years later. If we had chosen to leave that dreadful summer of 2000, what incredible blessings we would have missed out on.

Journaling Topic

What areas of your life require patience? How does Scripture help you see these areas from God's perspective?

Idea for Prayer

Pray for those who work in ministries that take patience. Pray they would be faithful to sow and then trust God for the harvest. Pray for the people of Japan to turn to Christ.

Holly Ann Bell (1995) is married to Patrick Bell. Both received their MAs in Intercultural Studies from Wheaton College. They met smuggling Bibles into Eastern Europe in 1989 while serving with International Teams. They have three children, all born in Hagi, Japan. They own and operate two English conversation schools in Japan.

KAZAKHSTAN

When you open up to someone

. . . .

Marina and Fish

Paige Buzbee Pushkin

Traditional Kazak cuisine always gives preference to boiled foods and the use of milk and milk products. Meat serves as the basis of the majority of meals. *Piroshki* are a food common in Kazakhstan that originated in Russia. This is a small Russian turnover made of a pastry wrapped around various fillings such as meat, seafood, cheese and mushrooms. *Piroshki* can be baked or fried and are often served as hors d'oeuvres or to accompany soups and salads. A *pirogi* is a larger version of *piroshki* and is served as the main entrée.

Scripture – Psalm 31:20a
In the shelter of your presence you hide them...

Story

I had already been in Kazakhstan for two years. The winter stretched almost endlessly for a girl from Miami, Florida, and I was tired of living in the fish bowl called "missions." I felt torn between wanting desperately to go back to my mother's house in Georgia and being absolutely petrified at the thought of leaving the new life God had built for me in this former Soviet country.

On Wednesday, May 1, my friend Marina and I perched on chairs in her kitchen; sunlight and cool air came in through the open window. I was there to learn how to make *piroshki*. The last time we had been together was during my dad's visit in early April so we had a lot of catching up to do. After covering the basics—her family and studies, my classes, life in general—we moved on to deeper topics.

I told her I would be going to the village of Sergeyvka, where one of my teammates lived and ministered, in the coming week for a rest. I admitted to her that I had not been feeling like myself lately. As she listened, I shared with her things God had been teaching me through my struggles about who he was and about his character. I had been reading a book about the names of God and had come across a verse that had remained close to my heart: "You hide them [those who come to God for protection] in the shelter of your presence…" (Ps. 31:20). I explained to Marina that God's presence, which is so real to me when I pray, is my shelter, my hiding place, from difficulties.

Like the analogy of a fish in water, God is always as close as our next breath. I admitted to her that sometimes I get into trouble or get discouraged because I forget his presence is so near. Marina sat still and listened intently, hanging on every word I uttered. When I finished she admitted that no one had ever talked to her so personally and naturally about the things of God. She said, "Paige, no one, not even my parents when I was a child, has ever talked to me about God the way you do. When I pray I think of him as far away from me, up in the heavens—now I will try to think of him the way you explained him to me."

Marina called me the next night full of enthusiasm and excitement: "Paige, I just wanted to tell you good night. I smiled all day after being with you last night. It was not only rest for my body but rest for my soul." After we hung up I sat marveling at the seemingly backward way God had reached my friend through my struggle. Isn't it like him to use my weakness to glorify himself? As one of my favorite songs says, "Your kingdom is established as I live to know you more." Even though I still felt tired and looked forward to the coming retreat at my teammate's home, I found that I too had been refreshed at Marina's place as we talked of God in such a natural manner about how she could experience the "shelter of his presence" in a personal way.

Journaling Topic

Are you willing to share your struggles and weaknesses with others? If not, what holds you back?

Idea for Prayer

Pray for Marina and her relationship with God. Ask God to help you be transparent with others.

Paige Buzbee Pushkin *(2003) served with The Mission Society of United Methodists for over two years in Karaganda, Kazakhstan where she taught intermediate English eight times a week to teenagers and adults. She has also taught English to refugees and immigrants in the United States through World Relief. Currently she is the administrator of a program for refugees in Atlanta, Georgia, where she lives with her husband Andrej.*

KENYA

When listening to the words of the wise

. . . .

Grandpa Isindeli

Barbara Miner Collins

Located in the eastern part of Africa, Kenya is often referred to as the land of the safari. The yearly migration of wildlife between Serengeti National Park in Tanzania and Maasai Mara National Park in Kenya rates as one of nature's greatest attractions. The animal trek has been captured by filmmakers worldwide. Kenya's most common large carnivore is the spotted hyena. Often thought of as timid and cowardly, the hyena can be extremely dangerous and aggressive. Its Swahili name is *Fisi* and its eerie cry is heard in the night across the northern frontier.

Scripture – John 14:6
…*"I am the way, and the truth and the life. No one comes to the Father except through me."*

Story
When we first arrived in Kenya after finishing three months of language school, we received assignment to a former famine relief camp in the northern frontier. Families debilitated by famine lived around the edge of the "mission station," and my first impression reminded me of an old Western movie I had seen—the Indian tents surrounding "the post."

In time, an elderly male came to be my houseman. Although he could not read or write, I remain convinced that he is the most spiritual person I have ever met. His name was Grandpa Isindelli. A neighboring tribe grabbed Grandpa during his youth while he guarded the herds. They quite literally carved him up and left him for dead. He survived because of the mission station. His injuries were such that he could never have children. However, his children became a matter of tribal arrangement, and he took them as his own. Eventually he became a Christian.

One night Grandpa's only son, a boy we would consider physically challenged, struggled with malaria. Grandpa Isindelli sat by his side since the child had been taking a lot of chloroquine. (Chloroquine is a drug used to prevent and treat malaria—a red blood cell infection transmitted by the bite of a mosquito.) The next morning Grandpa told us this story:

"As I sat next to my son, listening to the sounds of the night, I heard a hyena crying out, '*Arume! Arume! Arume!*' (*Arume* means truth.) Those who are lost without Christ are like the hyena, wandering and calling, 'Truth, truth, truth.' Jesus said, 'I am the way and the truth and the life.'"

Many nights I too have listened to the sounds of the dark and remembered this story. Like Grandpa Isindelli, I sought to hear God's voice sending me truth in whatever situation I currently faced. I know that many others cry out "truth, truth, truth" as well. As a Christian, I want to listen and respond to that cry—offering God's truth freely in Jesus Christ our Lord.

Journaling Topic

When you lie awake at night, what do you hear? How does Grandpa Isindelli's story impact you? What truth is God speaking to you currently?

Idea for Prayer

Pray for the people of Kenya who have yet to hear and respond to God's truth offered in his son Jesus Christ. Pray for those who suffer, hunger and thirst due to famine across the northern portion of Africa.

Barbara Miner Collins (1995) spent twenty-five years in Kenya with Africa Inland Mission (AIM). She served on the northern frontier, along with her husband, translating the Bible. She also developed inner-city home visitations in Nairobi with the aid of a Kenyan missionary wife. Afterwards the family relocated to Eldoret where they assisted in the establishment of the founding faculty of the AIC Missionary College. There Barbara became director of the Women's Project, and later, the finance director. She and her husband now serve in Minneapolis reaching out to immigrants.

LIBERIA

When unexpected opportunities arise

. . . .

Unexpected Windows
of Opportunity

Ruth Maxwell

Located on the western coast of Africa, between Guinea, the Ivory Coast and Sierra Leone, Liberia is Africa's oldest republic. Founded by freed American and Caribbean slaves, indigenous African tribes make up ninety-five percent of its population. Since the exile of its former president in 2003, Liberia has been in the slow process of social and economic reconstruction. Due to its rich natural inheritance, the land stars as a major exporter of rubber, coffee, cocoa and timber. Its borders embrace some of Africa's largest and purest rain forests.

Scripture – Ephesians 2:10

For we are God's workmanship, created in Christ Jesus to do good works which God prepared in advance for us to do.

Story

While preparing to leave for home assignment at the end of my first term as a missionary, a dear Lebanese friend presented me with several gifts. I thanked her for her generosity and said that I would pack the gifts so that I could enjoy them upon my return. "No, take them with you," she cried. "You are not coming back!" Her response startled me, but before long I knew that she was right. I had planned on remaining in Liberia for decades just as my parents had, but my time abruptly ended after three years. The civil war robbed me of every expectation I had about my career in missions—or so I thought. Now that I've had time to mull over my experiences, God has been able to show me all of the unexpected windows of opportunity he provided in those three years.

During those three years in Liberia, I had the opportunity to minister in the capital city of Monrovia. From businessmen's wives and diplomats of all faiths to slum children and Turkish prostitutes, I found myself leading Bible studies and building friendships with women of all walks of life. I learned that, regardless of where they are from, women everywhere have much in common. Working in the business and diplomatic community opened ministry opportunities just as much as my outreach among the poor. An American Embassy liaison officer learned that I occasionally ran missionary kid re-entry programs for families going back to their passport countries, and wondered if I would be willing to do the same for embassy children returning to the US. After learning that I frequently provided tours of Monrovia for newcomers, I was asked if I would provide a city tour for the captain of a US Naval ship. The opportunities go on and on.

One situation particularly stands out. I met a woman by the name of Cecilia. She wanted to learn how to disciple, and I wanted to work with someone who wanted to learn how to disciple, so we knew God had arranged our relationship. Each week I met with Cecilia to develop culturally appropriate discipleship material for the Liberian context. Little did I know that the fruit of those times together would be born into the context of a war-torn city. With the little mentoring I had offered, Cecilia discipled people from tribes on either side of the conflict—working out her relationships in the anguished context of war, starvation and violence.

Our usual meeting place was a tiny coffee shop on Tubman Boulevard in Monrovia. In a city without phones, and with unreliable taxis, unrest and heavy rainfall that could bog traffic down, there were days when neither one of us made it on time. In case of a no-show, I always came with something extra to work on. On those days, God gave me an unexpected opportunity to slowly build a friendship with the Turkish woman who ran the café and one of her friends. Eventually, they invited me into their homes and we became friends. Outings with them introduced me to their perspective on Liberian life, which I could never have otherwise gained.

Yet the most remarkable unexpected window of opportunity was the invitation to teach English to a couple moving from Monrovia to Nairobi, Kenya. The three of us covered a number of topics in our English development conversations, including life-stories. Upon hearing my testimony, the ambassador's wife wondered why I felt no bitterness toward God. When I told her, "Yes, life could be hard, but God always saw me through," she looked surprised and remarked, "You really mean that, don't you?" Two years later, when I knocked on the embassy door in Nairobi, I asked for the ambassador by name, and was escorted to his inner office. "I thought you must have died in Liberia!" was all he could say, as we embraced. A week later I arrived for an arranged meeting with his wife; this was one week before the Gulf War began. This time of serious concern for them gave us much to talk about. It seemed that our paths had crossed again at just the right time.

When I look back on these amazing windows of opportunity, I remember how I had deeply longed to be a wise steward of whatever God placed before me. I had come to Liberia with expectations, but God had done something with me that I never could have expected. Although I had at first felt robbed, I gradually began to see the extraordinary opportunities God had provided me. Just because he hadn't given me foresight didn't mean that I hadn't been fulfilling his purposes. Did the war in Liberia rob me of a stable extended missionary experience? Perhaps, but if I was robbed, I was given so much more in return. Now I see that fulfilling his expectations is so much more rewarding than fulfilling my own.

Journaling Topic

What unexpected windows of opportunity have you had in the past few months?

Idea for Prayer

Pray for missionary women to be open to teaching and building relationships with women in all walks of life. Pray specifically for young women discipling those in the context of war, as well as for diplomatic women living cross-culturally.

Ruth Maxwell (1990) served in Liberia, Kenya, Angola and Canada. Her works include teaching Bible in a public school in Liberia, leading Bible studies, providing a home away from boarding school for missionary kids, doing missionary care, participating in the training of and development of missionaries and missionary caregivers and offering hospitality.

MEXICO

When you have to wait

. . . .

Waiting for Mr. Right

Tracey Moore Pieters

Mexico City ranks as one of the world's largest megalopolises with a population of more than twenty-six million. This "concrete jungle" teems with hungry souls. Although the Church has seen significant expansion in recent years, it cannot keep up with the population growth: less than three percent are evangelical Christians. With over half of the population under the age of fifteen, an entire generation waits to hear the gospel of the risen Christ.

Scripture – Psalm 37:4

> *Delight yourself in the Lord and he will give you the desires of your heart.*

Story

I was only a junior in college when I first came to Mexico. Although God had made it abundantly clear that he wanted me in Mexico that summer, I did have one ulterior motive: I hoped to win the attention of a missions-minded male friend. I figured that if I could get the missionary "call," maybe that friend would take more interest in me. The call came—from an amazing short-term program called Spearhead. They offered me an opportunity to live with a Mexican family, learn Spanish through immersion, minister alongside a local evangelical church and train with dedicated, more seasoned missionaries. As time unfolded,

God turned my world upside-down and revealed that he had a future for me in missions.

Upon my return to college, I anticipated a romance in my near future—one that involved a joint venture in missions. Instead I discovered that my "friend" had found his future wife that summer on another missions project. Through that heartache, God showed me all the more that my call was to missions—with or without a husband.

After my senior year I returned to Mexico for what I thought would be a one-year stint—to get missions "out of my system" before going on with my career plans. As it happened, God's plans looked different. Six weeks after my arrival, Mexico City suffered the devastating effects of two huge earthquakes—and I was right in the middle of the chaos. Ministering to families who had lost everything and sharing in the suffering of my host family and country, I felt such a deep tie to the Mexican people that I knew God had me right where he wanted me to be. So I asked God, "How can I serve you in such a huge, crowded, dangerous city all by myself? Please give me a husband who shares this vision you've given me." I was serving, but I was still single.

In the years that followed, I had several serious relationships, but it seemed that in each case marrying would mean having to leave my missionary calling or my beloved Mexico. Once, I came very close to accepting an attractive proposal that would have meant financial security and a cozy home in suburban America, but I had no peace in my heart. I asked God, "How can this be your will for my life if it feels like I am betraying the call that you have given me?" I had to say no. And so my wait continued—for ten years.

Occasions arose when I was tempted to go and look for a husband, but during those times I recalled Helen Rooseveare's story. She realized that her headlong pursuit of a husband on her first furlough was an act of disobedience (and she never married). Instead, I said to God, "Lord, I will continue serving you here where you have called me, and will trust that if you want to give me a husband, you can bring him to Mexico City." God's Word answered me with this assurance, "Delight yourself in the Lord and he will give you the desires of your heart."

One day a single missionary arrived on the field with another mission board and walked into the Spearhead office. His name was John Pieters. I didn't know in that moment that he was to be my future husband, but months later when we started a serious courtship, he said to me, "Tracey, when I came to Mexico this time, it was to spend my life here. How would you feel about spending the next twenty-five years of your life here with me?" I burst into a smile. My heart knew then that God had brought us together—two people with the same calling. We married a few months later.

Waiting for "Mr. Right" was not easy. Nor, in my case, was it a short wait. But, oh, was it worth it! God knew just the man I needed and brought him to me in his perfect timing. Our shared vision and love for Mexico showed only confirmation of what our souls already knew—that for both of us, God had given us the desires of our hearts.

Journaling Topic

What prayer are you waiting for God to answer? How can you delight yourself in the Lord while you wait for him?

Idea for Prayer

Pray for single missionaries that they would be secure in their call and wait on God's timing for issues of the heart.

Tracey Moore Pieters (1990) served in Latin America for nearly twenty years. For fifteen of those years she worked in leadership for Latin America Mission's Spearhead program, a unique mission training experience for young adults. The past five years, she and her husband John have planted churches among the neediest parts of Mexico. Her ministry has included teaching, discipling, counseling, administration, mentoring, leading Bible studies, hospitality and, most recently, home schooling her two daughters, Keila and Kiana.

MIDDLE EAST
When darkness breaks

. . . .

Aisha

Mary

Encompassed by mountains, seas and deserts, this region stands at the crossroads of Africa, Asia and Europe. As the birthplace of three major world religions, Judaism, Christianity and Islam, the Middle East brims with fascinating archaeology. In fact, it makes a good case for being the "cradle of civilization," especially with evidence of sophisticated societies like the ancient kingdoms of Persia, Babylon, Phoenicia and Egypt. These numerous and distinct countries may account for both its diverse cultures and the frequent cases of political and religious turmoil situated within its borders.

Scripture – Psalm 107:13-15
Then they cried to the Lord in their trouble, and he saved them from their distress. He brought them out of darkness and the deepest gloom and broke away their chains. Let them give thanks to the Lord for his unfailing love and his wonderful deeds for men.

Story
With an edgy bitterness in her voice, my orphan friend Aisha announced, "Lord willing, one day you will open the newspaper and read that I have died." She elaborated. "I want to die—to kill myself. I hate everybody and everybody hates me. I hate my life. There is nothing good in it. Everything is not beautiful," she emphasized in Arabic.

I sat across the tiny round table, stunned—unable to continue eating my schwarma sandwich as it lodged in my throat. Anger rose within me, and I could feel the heat spread over my face. How could life have already wearied my young friend in such a way? I wanted to yell, scream, kick and cry because of the effect of sin in this world. How could her mom and dad have abandoned this beautiful girl as a baby? How could people make her feel so unwanted and unloved? How could she feel hopeless, dreamless and desperate at only seventeen?

Quickly I composed myself. I didn't want to waste this opportunity by being angry. Instead I needed to use it to share about the hope that comes from knowing the love of God. Aisha and I spent the next forty-five minutes talking about pain, and the holes we have in our hearts because of this broken world. I confided in her about the ways that I have tried to fill my own heart, but how I have nothing in this life that satisfies me like God does. With both elbows on the table and her chin resting on her fists, my Muslim friend leaned in closer to me, nodding her head—seemingly relating to everything I said. "Nothing," I repeated, "nothing will fill your heart like God will."

Then I quoted to her the verses from Jeremiah 29:12-13. I told her that it is written in the Holy Book that if we look for God with our whole heart, we will find him. She shivered and grew excited as I spoke these words. "But you must look for him with your whole heart, not just part of it," I stressed. Slapping her hands on the table, she shouted, "I want that book! I want to read that book! Can you get one for me?" My jaw nearly dropped open in amazement.

The next time I visited the orphanage, Aisha showed no interest in small talk. She grabbed some chairs, pushed me into one and immediately began talking about God. Within minutes several of the other teenage girls gathered around to join in our discussion. "Mary, I want you to become a Muslim," Aisha stated assertively. "I want to be with you in heaven." Remembering the words of a friend of mine, I smiled and said, "Aisha, I have everything I need in Jesus." She smiled back and pondered my response for a moment. Then she suggested, "Maybe we can read you a story out of the Qu'ran and you can read us a story out of the Bible." I readily agreed and Aisha scampered off to get her Qu'ran.

After she returned and finished reading her story to the rest of the girls and me, she and her friends pleaded for me to read to them from the Bible. Miraculously the director of the orphanage gave us permission, so I opened my Arabic-English version to the Psalms. For the next fifteen minutes I listened to a Muslim orphan read to us the Psalmist's words in Arabic. She read of the unfailing love of God. As I listened, I marveled at the way God makes a way for such impossible opportunities. Noticing Aisha's eyes, I realized they no longer darkened with misery and despair. They flashed bright with hope and expectation. It seems there is a future, as God's Word says—even for this young orphaned girl named Aisha.

Journaling Topic

What do you think it would be like to be a female orphan in the Middle East? What experience have you had with orphans in your own context?

Idea for prayer

Pray for Aisha and her friends in the orphanage in the Middle East. Pray for workers like Mary who bring them hope through visits, friendship and the love of God.

Mary (2002) (pseudonym) works with community development projects in the Middle East. The main focuses of her ministry are women and children.

MONGOLIA

When actions speak louder than words

. . . .

The Power of Laughter

Kristy McGarvey

Bordered on the north by Russia and on the southeast and west by China, Mongolia lies in the heart of the Asian continent. The absolute magnitude and beauty of the Mongolian scenery intertwines with their nomadic lifestyle and renowned hospitality. One of the few countries in our century which has managed to retain its ancient traditions and culture, Mongolia only recently emerged from Communism in the 1990s. It is still a country searching for its identity. Although Buddhism ranks as the dominant religion, many people still live in a hopeless state of atheism.

Scripture – John 3:30

He must become greater; I must become less.

Story

It's not often that I wake up in the morning dreading the day ahead, but this morning seemed unlike many in my life for I was not in the land of my birth. I was in Mongolia, and on that particular day I was to attend a picnic by the river. All of the Sunday school teachers from the region of churches we'd been working with would be there. The last few days they had been our "students," but today we would all simply be "friends."

Almost immediately upon my arrival to Mongolia, we received our first assignment. The plan included coming up with a full three-day seminar to train the primary teachers for the church's educational ministry program. The job may not have been daunting under different circumstances, but what were four unprepared, young English-speaking women going to tell people who probably had more years of experience than we did in our life? Not to mention, they thought and spoke in a completely different language than my own.

In spite of our incompetence in communication with the people, lack of knowledge about the culture and inability to speak their language, we somehow made it through the first two days—albeit a bit frustrated. A long pause followed every sentence I spoke, so the translator could communicate my thoughts. This seemed perhaps the most difficult activity to bear. For the first time I realized how much I depended on my ability to use words and emotions to move people's hearts. In this situation, all of my skill proved irrelevant. For all I could tell, my thoughts may have vanished somewhere along the road of translation. But today I would not be in a classroom, and I so desperately wanted to love and care for these people. How could I show them that love fully without using words?

The day dazzled. Summer in Mongolia brings blue skies stretching from horizon to horizon. Arriving at the river, we greeted each other with smiling faces and grasping hands. All of the teachers seemed so excited to have us and wanted to make sure we became a part of the games.

Before long, we dashed about playing some form of tag. If I could have stepped back and watched myself from a distance, I'm sure I would have been a sorry sight. Throughout the day I tried one game after another without understanding the rules. To my relief, the warm air began to draw people to take a dip in the river. I felt relieved, that is until I saw how mucky it was. No way was I going in there! Reluctantly, however, I joined the group. The day beamed so hot, and they actually looked like they were having fun. I soon found myself immersed in water battles and swimming lessons—but that's not what surprised me most.

Before my eyes, I found myself communicating with people from another culture. I don't know why I hadn't thought of it before, but we were communicating by action instead of word. Together we shared experiences that we both understood. These became the beginning stages of a relationship. I had depended on my faculty of speech so strongly that I hadn't realized how God had equipped me to love others through my actions. As I played and laughed with these people, I stopped focusing on my own abilities and skills. The Lord gently reminded me that my being in Mongolia—or anywhere for that matter—was about his work. He would find a way to care for them through me if I would just let him. Although learning a people's verbal language ranks as a high priority for missionary work, I now realize that we have a universal language. Communication and ministry can begin long before the words come when we learn to act in love and laughter.

Journaling Topic

What are the faculties that you depend on to communicate and to validate your ability? Why are those abilities so important to you? How can you give those over to God's control?

Idea for Prayer

Pray for missionaries who are in the midst of language study and find themselves frustrated with their inability to fully minister to the people whom they are called to. Pray for encouragement and constant surrender to God's work in their lives, as well as in the lives of those they work with. Pray that God might give them opportunities to show love through action until they learn the language and culture of the people.

Kristy McGarvey *(2006) has an MA in Missions and Intercultural Studies from Wheaton College. She plans to train and teach church leaders—equipping them to lead their congregations. Kristy grew up as a missionary kid in the Philippines, but she had the opportunity of traveling to Mongolia. Along with three other women, she spent a short-term summer internship working in the children's programs and training teachers at a local church.*

MOROCCO
When being is enough

. . . .

Roses to Smell

Kimberly Wenger Sanford

Morocco sits strategically placed on the coastlines of North Africa, with its southeast situated in the Western Sahara desert. It is home to the largest city in North Africa—Casablanca, an economic center. Morocco possesses a rich culture stemming from Arab, Berber, European and African influences. As you walk through the open-air markets piled with rugs, jewelry and art, the strong smell of spices permeates the air. Known for sweet mint tea and traditional storytelling music, its indigenous people are referred to as "the Berbers." Morocco literally means, "the land of God"—ninety-eight percent of the population is Muslim.

Scripture – Luke 1:45
Blessed is she who has believed that what the Lord has said to her will be accomplished!

Story
Because Village of Hope (VOH) seemed concerned more with the quality of life over the quantity of accomplishments, I chose their organization's internship program. They encourage their interns to enter fully into a new culture in order to become learners. Over and over again they urged me to "just be" instead of incessantly trying to find something to do. Yet, despite the injunctions about not gaining my sense of worth through my work, about four months into my internship I hit a

crisis point. My English students couldn't speak any better than they did when I arrived, the public libraries I had planned to start weren't even close to being ready and my Arabic language skills didn't amount to much. "What had I been doing for the past four months?" I began asking myself.

The realization that so many of my expected accomplishments remained undone contributed to my rapidly increasing self-doubt. I viewed my internship as a failure; I didn't even have the language skills to explain to my host sister why I always returned home sad. But what really affected my spirits was the fact that I felt like I was losing touch with God. I continued down that path, passing in and out of something near depression over the course of what felt like many, many weeks.

Then one evening I went home to find my host mother Fatima sitting on the ground in the kitchen (a little concrete room detached from the main house) cracking walnuts. When I went in to join her, I sat down and picked up a rock. Fatima and I remained seated in that dim little kitchen for close to three hours, repeatedly crushing the outer shell of the nuts and picking out the edible meat. What amazed me about this evening was that Fatima barely spoke a word of Arabic. She never went to school as a girl, so she knew only the tribal dialect spoken in the mountains by her family group. I had learned only about three words of their dialect since the rest of the family spoke Arabic fluently. Yet in those several hours we found things to laugh about; we both tried to tell stories (although we knew the other would not understand). We simply enjoyed each other's company. Once the work ended I had proved that I was the worst walnut-cracker in the Middle Atlas Mountains. But Fatima didn't care. Apparently, we both benefited from those hours of "just being" together; our relationship changed after that evening.

Since then God has helped me to develop my vision for future ministry. I plan to return to Morocco in the near future, but not necessarily as a teacher or a developmental aid worker or in any other full-time occupation. I now have a desire to simply live in another culture as a neighbor, as a friendly face and as a warm and welcoming Christian individual who invests my time in any relationships God brings my way.

Journaling Topic

When was the last time you took time to just be with a friend? How did this impact your relationship?

Idea for Prayer

Pray for cross-cultural workers who are preparing to serve abroad.

Kimberly Wenger Sanford (2005) interned in rural Morocco as an ESL teacher immersed in the Village of Hope (VOH), a home for abandoned children. She taught English to the primarily non-literate women who worked as VOH's kitchen staff, as well as to several groups of high school students and recent graduates in a nearby village. She teaches English to refugees and is the training director for Via Terra, an intercultural business training organization. She lives in the Chicago area with her husband.

PAKISTAN
When the Spirit leads

. . . .

The Passenger

Ginny Feldman

Pakistan, an Islamic country located in southern Asia, borders Iran and Afghanistan to the west, China to the northeast and India to the east. It is the site of some of the earliest human settlements. For example, the ancient city of Moenjodara located on the west bank of the Indus River is more than five thousand years old. This city was discovered and excavated in 1922. Exposed to high temperature and excessive moisture, the conservation of this ancient city has become a concern of the government and other conservation groups worldwide.

Scripture — Acts 17:27

God did this so that men would seek him and perhaps reach out for him and find him, though he is not far from each one of us.

Story

Often, traveling in Pakistan provides unique opportunities for witness. One such incident stands out in my mind as a stark reminder that God can transcend cultural taboos when he wants someone to hear about himself.

I was flying from Lahore to Islamabad in the evening and a thunderstorm developed along the way. The wind and rain lashed at our plane and lightning and thunder frightened all the passengers. Once in awhile the plane seemed to freefall a couple of hundred feet and then keep going. There were no announcements from airhostesses or the captain, only the eerie feeling that we flew in mortal danger. I had flown all my life but never had I experienced a flight like this one! You could have heard a pin drop in that cabin.

I could see many passengers saying their *namaz* (Koranic prayers) or reciting the names of Allah using their prayer beads. The young man next to me said his *namaz*. The little girl on the other side grew sleepy and scared, so I comforted her and she fell asleep. I took out my Bible and began reading and praying, "OK, Lord, if this is the time you're calling me home, I'm ready." The Lord did comfort me through his Word and his Spirit.

After some twenty minutes of turbulence, our plane pulled through the storm and we began flying normally. By this time, only ten minutes remained of the flight.

"Please, could you tell me what you were reading?" asked the polite young man beside me.

"My Bible," I replied.

"Oh! I've always wanted one of those!" he exclaimed.

"Here, take it," and I showed him a couple of places he could start reading and explained just a bit about Jesus before the plane landed. Later, I stood amazed that I so easily gave him my personal, precious Bible. But we had such a close brush with death that hanging on to it obsessively didn't seem important anymore.

I never saw him again but have often prayed for him—the polite, anonymous passenger—to come to repentance and faith in Jesus Christ.

I still marvel at how God seated that young man right next to someone (perhaps the only person on the plane) who had a Bible, and proceeded to give us enough of a jolt that we would trespass the cultural norm of not speaking with someone of the opposite gender. He arranged it all so that a hungry heart could receive some heavenly manna.

Truly, God is sovereign and he cares. He is not far from each one of us (Acts 17:27) and rewards those who earnestly seek him (Heb. 11:6).

Journaling Topic

When have you been presented with a unique opportunity to witness?

What cultural norms were involved, if any?

Idea for Prayer

Pray for the Pakistani passenger (and people) to understand the truth that is revealed in the Bible.

Ginny Feldmann (1995) served in Pakistan with SIM International for eighteen years in Christian education among children, young girls and women as well as evangelistic outreach among the Riasiti people group. She also served on the SIM Pakistan Council as personnel manager and newcomer coordinator. Currently she works with SIM in the Chicago (Illinois) area, in outreach to South Asians and in seeking to motivate local churches to engage in ethnic outreach in their communities.

PAPUA NEW GUINEA
When your faith is tested

. . . .

Restrictions

Sarita Dolores Gallagher

According to *Operation World*, Papua New Guinea ranks ethnically and linguistically as the world's most complex nation. Although the official language is English, over eight hundred other languages are spoken by the diverse population. Well known for its beautiful flora and fauna, which includes "the bird of paradise," rugged terrain complicates the management of the nation's rich natural resources, such as timber, oil and gas.

Scripture – James 1:2-4

Consider it pure joy, my brothers, whenever you face trials of many kinds, because you know that the testing of your faith develops perseverance. Perseverance must finish its work so that you may be mature and complete, not lacking anything.

Story

My heart sank as soon as the words came out of the pastor's mouth. Just days before my departure to Papua New Guinea (PNG) as a first-term missionary, what he had to say rated as the very last thing I wanted to hear. Nevertheless, there I slumped in my pew at church listening to his words: "Sarita, these verses in James 1:2-4 are from God, and they refer to your upcoming time in PNG."

I quickly flipped through the pages of my Bible to find the verse. The words on the page engulfed me—"trials of many kinds," "testing of your faith," "perseverance must finish its work?' My heart groaned, and I quickly cried out "Oh Lord, please, no more trials, struggles and pain!" Just a year and a half earlier, my Mum had passed away after a painful struggle with cancer. Just a few months after, my relatives underwent another family upheaval. "Maybe, just maybe," I thought hopefully, "the pastor is wrong. Yes, that must be it. Surely my experience won't be as bad as all that..."

Six months later I recalled that scene as I climbed determinedly up the dirt path of Bethel Center's aptly named, "Prayer Mountain." From the height of the small hill I could look down upon the swaying coconut trees, vegetable gardens and makeshift houses of the Port Moresby suburb of Tokarara. The beauty of the surroundings was, however, lost on me for my eyes fixed resolutely on the steep dusty path. Pain, frustration and agony seemed to pump through my veins—my heart felt as though it wanted to leap from my body. Over and over again the words, "I can't take it anymore," thumped through my head. After just half a year in the country I felt overcome with sheer desperation.

While in PNG I expected to encounter many cultural and language differences, but nothing had prepared me for the particular difficulty that awaited me in Port Moresby. While other parts of PNG are quite safe, Port Moresby and its surrounding neighborhoods are known as "high-risk locations." Armed robberies, car-jackings and sometimes even physical attacks are common. While most Papua New Guineans find relative safety in the city, foreigners tend to be targets. Needless to say, the very real dangers of living in the city greatly restricted my life. As a young white female, my movement was almost entirely limited to the Bible school property. For a woman who had previously trekked Europe alone, and whose favorite activities included running, hiking and traveling, these restrictions soon became unbearable.

Sitting among the branches of the tallest tree I could find, I ardently poured out my heart to God. The high barbed wire fence to my right enclosed the property. It taunted me, as though it was a picture of my physical representation of my present emotional condition. I felt trapped—trapped beyond anything I had experienced—beyond anything I had ever imagined. My Western upbringing encouraged independence and had ill-prepared me for a life on a two-acre campus. "God,"

I earnestly cried out, "from now on it has to be all. I have nothing left to give." My body slumped down as I let out this final plea for help. I've heard that everyone has a breaking point, and I just discovered mine. I had barely gotten out of bed the next morning when I suddenly heard a knock on the door of my small house. When it opened, the cheerful smile of one of our school's Filipino students greeted me. She explained that she had been thinking of me early that morning and wanted to know if I would like to attend an all-day barbeque with her. God heard my cry! Relief swept throughout my body. After having stayed on the school property almost continually for six months, God worked this small miracle before my very eyes.

Continued invitations from the Filipino Christian Fellowship followed and, shortly after, an evangelistic soccer team formed at the Bible school. Within a few days my previously nonexistent social schedule filled to capacity. I actually had to turn down some invitations. Although the restrictions of Port Moresby life continued, I learned that although pressure and trials abound on the mission field, so does God's love, mercy and provision.

Journaling Topic

How has God used a friend to help you through a transition?

Idea for Prayer

Pray for meaningful friendships for cross-cultural workers.

Sarita Dolores Gallagher *(2000) works with Christian Revival Crusade International in Port Moresby, Papua New Guinea. She holds an MA in Missions and Intercultural Studies and a BA in English Literature and Spanish Language and Literature. She is currently a doctoral student in missions at Fuller Theological Seminary.*

PHILIPPINES
When adopting children across cultures

. . . .

Becoming a Family

Nancy Kelley Alvarez

The Philippines are a chain of islands located off the coast of Southeast Asia, to the east of Vietnam. The climate is tropical marine and the land primarily mountainous. Filipino (based on Tagalog) and English are the two major languages spoken, and the majority of the people are Roman Catholic. The capital is Manila where Faith Academy, an international school, is located.

Scripture – Isaiah 58:7-9

Is it not to share your food with the hungry and to provide the poor wanderer with shelter—when you see the naked, to clothe him, and not to turn away from your own flesh and blood? Then your light will break forth like the dawn, and your healing will quickly appear; then your righteousness will go before you, and the glory of the Lord will be your rear guard. Then you will call, and the Lord will answer; you will cry for help, and he will say: "Here am I."

Story

Like many singles on the mission field, I struggled with loneliness. I found it difficult to find friends who could spend quality time with me after "work hours." So I was surprised at my response to the Filipino man from the school who asked me if I wanted to play tennis. The days grew so hot and he wanted to play so early in the morning. My love for sleep got the best of me. "No, thanks," I said. Thankfully, on the spur of the moment, I added, "But you can ask me again another time." And he did. This time, I realized the offer as an opportunity to make a new friend. Over time we found that we enjoyed talking together more than we enjoyed playing tennis

Instead of once a week, we started getting together twice a week for tennis. Then one day, I asked if I could come and hear him preach. Not long after, he spoke with a missionary friend of his about how to know if an American woman was interested in dating him or not. According to her advice, he decided to invite me out to something other than tennis. Our first excursion took us to a free concert at a nearby university. We shared many times together after that day.

One day I realized that this was the man God intended for me as a life partner. When he asked if I believed God was doing something special in our relationship, I said, "Yes, but I'm worried about the cross-cultural aspect." Gently he reminded me, "Perfect love casts out fear" (I John 4:18). And he was right. We realized that our different backgrounds enriched our relationship and caused us to work at our communication as a couple. After a series of delays, we got a visa for him to travel to the US for our wedding. While there we received enough support to continue our ministry at ISOT-Asia.

Since we were older, we decided to start a family early in our marriage. However, I felt sure that I would have difficulty in pregnancy due to previous medical problems. Indeed, we found that we could not have a baby. Adoption, it seemed, represented our only option.

While I was all for adoption my husband, who came from a very poor family, said, "I can't bear the thought of adopting a stranger's child when my own sister needs help raising her children." His sister, a single mother of five children, struggled daily to feed, clothe and provide basic necessities for them. She worked two jobs and was hardly ever home. Her youngest daughter was only five at the time. In response to his suggestion, I told him that I couldn't bear the thought of taking a woman's children from her and wondered if we couldn't send her money instead. But he knew that we could never send her enough money to meet their needs. What the children really needed were parents who would give them love and stability. After much prayer, the Lord finally gave me peace about this situation.

When we spoke to my sister-in-law, she proved willing to let us legally adopt two of her children. We all agreed that it would be best to adopt the two youngest children, Paul John and Marian. Due to unforeseen circumstances we could not visit them until the following Christmas. This gave me time to research books and talk to others about adopting older children. As the time drew near so did my anticipation to bring the children home. I realized that God had been preparing me inwardly, giving me a deeper love for Paul John and Marian.

As I look back on this incredible journey, I have to say we have had our frustrations and challenges. However, we trudge along slowly, making progress spiritually and emotionally as we become a family. I've learned that God is always with me. He orchestrates the events of my life—even when I'm naïve enough to enter into the adoption of two older children from another culture. Although my decisions may not always be the right ones at the right time, he uses them and guides me through my choices. Through it all, I have realized my desperate need for him and have come to understand what it truly means for me to live by faith, both as a wife and as a mother of two beautiful children.

Journaling Topic

Who are some people in your life that you need to care for?

Idea for Prayer

Pray for the children in the Philippines as well as the missionary workers there.

Nancy Kelley Alvarez received her TESOL certificate from Wheaton College Graduate School and went to the Philippines to teach English as a Second Language at the International School of Theology (ISOT)—Asia. Started by Campus Crusade for Christ, ISOT emphasizes ministry skills and character development along with academic excellence. Nancy's work also includes mentoring women.

ROMANIA
When facing a fearful situation

. . . .

Helping Hands

Jennifer Hobday

Bordering the Black Sea of Southeastern Europe, located between Bulgaria and Ukraine, Romania is the largest of the Balkan countries. The Danube River runs freely throughout the country, forming the largest wetland in the world. With its rich and varied culture, Romania seems distinctly different from the rest of Europe. Although filled with stately castles, medieval towns and painted monasteries dating back to the fifteenth century, Romania transitioned out of communism as recently as 1989, and the country is slowly improving its economic and political footing.

Scripture – Psalm 27:1-2

The Lord is my light and my salvation—whom shall I fear? The Lord is the stronghold of my life—of whom shall I be afraid? When evil men advance against me to devour my flesh, when my enemies and my foes attack me, they will stumble and fall.

Story

I arrived at the schoolyard early one day. Everyday Teri, Wes and I carried responsibility for a small group of street boys. Grabbing pens and notebooks, we took the boys from the day center to a half-day school program across town, and then picked them up two hours later. That day Wes and Teri were scheduled to meet me right before the boys arrived. I glanced at my watch—11:30. Although the boys were due out of school at noon, the teacher often grew tired and let them out early. It became a daily struggle, not just to arrive on time without any fights or mishaps, but to know how to be more than a chaperone. These children grew up so differently than I had. What of their world could I understand? As I pondered this, my eyes followed a small child who ran toward the nearby park to play on the rusted swings and monkey bars.

Looking up from the boy, my eyes widened. In front of me stood a man—a man with rotten teeth. I noticed him earlier, watching me as I got off the tram. A swollen lump rose to my throat and I choked. He looked at me as though he knew me and said something I couldn't understand. Impolitely, I bowed my head.

He then stepped closer. His dark hair, uncombed and greasy, stuck to his scalp. He seemed to be asking for something. In fractured Romanian, I told him that I was waiting for my boyfriend—it was a lie, and not a very good one. Another grin spread across his face when he detected my foreignness. He took another step in my direction. His hot breath smelled foul and made my stomach turn. I tried to look beyond the man, in search of Wes or Teri or one of the boys, but saw only the empty street. Do I leave or do I stay? What does he want, anyway?

As the man continued to talk to me in a low-hushed tone, I tossed the questions back and forth in my mind, and subconsciously headed up the street toward a nearby market where I might find people. Forcing my eyes to stay on the road, I could hear his shoes hitting the pavement and scraping the gravel, not far behind me. Thump, scuffle, thump. The sound rang in my ears.

When he finally passed me, I released the breath I had been holding in my lungs. Suddenly he turned and motioned for me to follow him. My heart began to pound against my ribs. Was he just a nice man? I couldn't be certain.

Praying frantically, I turned back toward the school. He stopped and turned as well, and I hated myself for being afraid, for not knowing what to do. Out of the corner of my eye I spotted the "teachers only" entrance and begged my legs to carry me there. Ducking inside the building, I watched him pass. My body quivered slightly and I reached for the door handle to steady myself.

Longing only to return to the meeting point and find Wes, I slipped outside hastily. The corroded hinges of the metal door creaked and attracted the attention of this middle-aged man. He walked toward me once again. In desperation, I asked what he wanted—deciding that if it was my money, he could have it. Instead he made an inappropriate gesture and pulled out a sweaty wad of bills—thrusting them in my direction. I stood, paralyzed in horror, until the force that held me relented. I ran and ran and ran without uttering a word, until I hit the blue side of Wes's fleece coat. Without knowing why, he held me as I sobbed.

Finally the boys arrived, along with Teri, but I couldn't find the words in any language to express what had just happened. So I stood silently and then followed the group back to the bus, toward the day center. As I slumped in my seat, I realized that I had entered into some of the darkness that the boys faced daily—I hated it. Stepping off the bus, I was bombarded with children, but the anger and fear continued to wash over me.

As we walked toward the center, I stumbled over an uneven brick road—a messy construction project had buried it in mud. One of the boys, Miu, took my hand questioningly. His red pants were splattered with mud. "C'mon, Jen," was all he said, and the street child led the aid worker down the street past potholes and puddles. He stopped at a small bakery and, letting go of my hand, reached into his pocket for the only money he had to his name. Giving it to the owner in exchange for two cookies, he handed one to me. *"Pentru tine,"* he said. "For you." Then he took my hand to lead me home.

Journaling Topic

When was a time that you were afraid? How did God protect you?

Idea for Prayer

Pray for the street children of Romania and around the world.

Jennifer Hobday *(2005) was involved in a children's ministry focusing on street children in Galati, Romania. She became aware of the barriers due to language, culture and education. Currently, she teaches elementary education in a Christian school in Illinois and recently married.*

RUSSIA

When called to give an answer

. . . .

The Hope That We Have

Lisa Christian

The world's largest country by land area, Russia occupies much of Europe and all of North Asia. The climate in Russia varies from extreme cold in Northern Russia and Siberia to subtropical weather in the coastal areas of the Black Sea. More than sixty ethnic groups exist within the twenty-one republics of Russia. However, due to the antireligious ideology of the former Soviet government, most of these groups have no religious affiliation. Since the fall of the Soviet Union in 1991, the Russian Orthodox Church and other Christian churches have experienced growth.

Scripture – I Peter 3:15-17

But in your hearts set apart Christ as Lord. Always be prepared to give an answer to everyone who asks you to give the reason for the hope that you have. But do this with gentleness and respect, keeping a clear conscience, so that those who speak maliciously against your good behavior in Christ may be ashamed of their slander. It is better, if it is God's will, to suffer for doing good than for doing evil.

Story

"What is your purpose for being here? Is it teaching English or something else?" asked the government official who sat across the table looking straight at me with her piercing gaze. I knew it was the "something else" that gave pause to my response. In the brief uncomfortable silence that followed her question, I prayed silently for wisdom. How could I explain my purpose for being in this city?

Feeling somewhat unprepared in my answer I said, "I am a Christian and I work with my colleague here teaching English as a Foreign Language." Dissatisfied with my response, she posed more questions. When she inquired about my church affiliation, I responded, "Pentecostal," and that immediately set her off on a discourse about Russia's Orthodox tradition. What struck me the most was her suspicion of Christians in general. She seemed to believe that Americans and Christian English teachers "were not wanted or needed in her city."

As I listened to her lengthy speech I could not help but be reminded of the disciples in the book of Acts who so often stood before government and religious officials. They also heard that they were not wanted or needed. Suddenly the official gave my Russian colleague, Pastor Vladimir, a stern reprimand for allowing me to start a school and accused me of not teaching English but preaching the gospel. Even though he assured her that I taught only English in the classroom, she told us not to say anything about the Bible or Christianity in or out of the classroom. If I wanted to stay in this city, she strongly advised me "to teach English based on Russian culture, not American culture."

After the meeting, Pastor Vladimir, Sveta (my interpreter) and I prayed together. We discussed the meeting and, after reviewing our options, decided to continue with the school even though some negative consequences could result.

Since that meeting, the school has continued to grow. I continue to teach English in the classroom and train others to minister to our students. The Deputy Mayor has fought Vladimir on most projects, yet later has realized that they were needed. Although these are uncertain times for us, hope lives within the hearts of the believers in Russia. We have met with some opposition, but others have had more difficulty than we have had over the years. I feel privileged to work alongside committed believers like Pastor Vladimir and Sveta who truly exercise their faith and hope in the Lord Jesus Christ on a daily basis.

Journaling Topic

Have you faced harassment or difficulty because of your faith in Jesus Christ? If yes, how did you respond? If not, how would you respond?

Idea for Prayer

Pray earnestly for the pastors, churches and missionaries who face opposition for the sake of the gospel worldwide. Pray for Russian Christians, that they will be prepared to give an answer for the hope that dwells within them.

Lisa Christian *(2003) is an African-American who has taught English as a Foreign Language in Russia for eight years. At the request of a national church she also opened a school. In addition, she supervises and trains short-term English language teachers for an international agency that sends them to teach for several months each summer at various locations throughout the country.*

SIERRA LEONE

When you least expect it

. . . .

A Father Who Knows What You Need

Evvy Hay Campbell

This beautiful savanna teeming with wildlife lies along the western coast of Africa. Historically significant in its role at both the beginning and end of slave trade, the Sierra Leone of today is still recovering from a brutal ten-year civil war. The conflict resulted in tens of thousands of deaths, and the displacement of close to one-third of its population. Mostly Muslim, ninety percent of its inhabitants come from twenty native African tribes.

Scripture – Matthew 6:8b

For your Father knows what you need before you ask him.

Story

As director of nursing in the early 1980s at Kamakwie Wesleyan Hospital, I was responsible for the community health program and mimeographing the forms used on patient charts in the lab. In contrast to doing a bladder tap by lantern-light, or slowly titrating intravenous anti-venom into someone who had suffered a recent snakebite, mimeographing forms remained a necessary but mundane task. The hospital, 180 miles inland from the capital city of Freetown and forty miles south of the Guinea border, was located in a remote area of equatorial Sierra Leone on an old trade route that ran from the Atlantic Ocean all the way up to Timbuktu in Mali.

With sixty-eight beds, two missionary physicians, four registered nurses, and forty staff trained on site, the hospital typically logged 1,500 admissions, five hundred major surgeries, 1,500 minor procedures and cared for fifty thousand outpatients each year. On top of that, a budding community health program also required attention, so the pace often seemed frantic. The year-ahead planning that required keeping adequate supplies and medicines on hand commonly became frustrated by delayed international shipments or procedural boondoggles in customs. We lived "in the bush." Eight hours in the hospital van over deeply rutted roads, or thirteen hours riding in the back of a battered public transport track, lay between Kamakwie and the stores of Freetown. Mailbags arrived irregularly and, on occasion, only monthly. We had radio contact with other mission stations twice each day, and gleaned news of the outside world via BBC or Voice of America.

One stifling afternoon, after drawing up a form for a new community health center opening the following day, I found that we had little paper left in the hospital storage cabinet. To make copies of the form I needed to find more. Hurrying across to the dispensary, I dug into the shipping cartons piled against the wall of the pharmacy storage room. Out of the eleven boxes I found healthy quantities of clinic registration tickets and the 5x8 cards used in the outpatient dispensary, but no mimeograph paper. Frustrated, I asked Dr. Pierson, the chief medical officer who happened to be there at the time, where the paper could be. He said that Dr. Paine had ordered some and I might find it in the bottom of the cartons. Having already restacked the boxes, I pulled them down a second time to search, but none held the paper I needed. Stymied and concerned, I put the boxes back and fell silent. A trip to Freetown was clearly out of the question.

Puzzling over what to do about the copies needed for the next day, I noticed the younger brother of one of the dispensers standing in the doorway—the glare of the afternoon sun silhouetting his slender figure. He had waited, courteous and silent, while Dr. Pierson and I talked and rummaged through the boxes. The young man introduced himself and told us that he had presently come from a conversation with some of the small traders just over the Guinea border. He told us that in the future the traders would have some items that we commonly needed at the hospital, such as paperclips and rubber bands. Apologizing that he didn't have any of those things with him, he extended both hands—as is customary when offering something to another—and said, "Today I have only this." In his outstretched hands rested a package of mimeograph paper!

A number of years have passed since that afternoon, but I still remember it clearly. What had made the experience so indelible was the specificity of it all. Compared to the extensive and commonly urgent work of the hospital, a package of mimeograph paper represented a small and ordinary item indeed. The improbability, however, of being presented with the needed paper at that particular moment, and in that isolated place, seemed truly extraordinary. Such a provision could only come from a Father who knows exactly what we need, precisely when we need it most.

Journaling Topic

Thank God for the times when he met your needs in unexpected ways. List five or six of these.

Idea for Prayer

Pray for doctors, nurses and hospital personnel who are under-resourced, that their needs will be met.

Evvy Hay Campbell (1996) served two terms with the Wesleyan Church in Sierra Leone, West Africa as director of Nursing at Kamakwie Wesleyan Hospital. She subsequently worked nine years with MAP International, a Christian relief and development agency, serving as director of International Health. Since 1996 Evvy has been on the Intercultural Studies faculty of Wheaton College.

SOUTH AFRICA
& SWAZILAND

When the task is overwhelming

. . . .

Turning the Tide—
Is It Possible?

Brenda Bagley

South Africa is celebrating over a decade of democracy since the end of apartheid in 1994. Many good changes have come, such as a constitution that values equality and opportunity for all its citizens. On the downside, the country struggles with the highest number of people with HIV/AIDS in the world, more than five million people.[1]

Scripture – John 10:10
> The thief comes only to steal and kill and destroy; I have come that they may have life, and have it to the full.

Story

The Church worldwide to a large extent seems reluctant to grapple with the issues of the day, and often opposes taking life-changing action that can begin to turn the tide of the evils of the time. Similarly, many church leaders of South Africa and Swaziland would like to hide their head in the sand when it comes to recognizing, acknowledging and acting to resolve the root problems of HIV/AIDS and sexual abuse that are destroying their nations.

Moses, a Tsonga-speaking high-school teacher who serves also as a church leader, invited Compassionate Ministries Southern Africa (CMSA) to teach pastors and leaders in his area. As the HIV/AIDS education team of CMSA traveled six hours to the Mpumalanga province in northeastern South Africa, they prayed about the ministry entrusted to them during the weekend that lay ahead.

The team had some surprises coming as they arrived to teach about HIV/AIDS, sexuality God's way, counseling and facilitating church leaders in finding ways that they can make a difference. About twenty people sat or stood around waiting for things to begin. The team noticed that the people were not smiling, shaking hands or extending the usual warm African welcoming gestures. Others slowly gathered in. It seemed a rather icy welcome in the warmth of an African summer. The team had not anticipated being unwelcome.

The meeting began with each team member presenting the material in a variety of ways. The people knew about the problem of AIDS. Many had experienced firsthand the trauma and death in their families, but it was taboo to talk about it. It loomed as a frightening dark problem associated with promiscuity. They thought that judgment represented the only appropriate response.

This day they faced some surprises. They heard about how Jesus offered compassion to the outcasts of society, to the promiscuous and the hopeless. Jesus offered forgiveness and hope of a new life. A visible thaw began to take place in the faces and responses of the women and men present that day. They began to ask questions burning in their hearts. Their confidence grew as they began to answer their own questions. The light of hope started shining in their eyes.

At the end of the day many rose to their feet and offered words of thanks to the team for coming. They were beginning to see they could do something to stop this terrible disease that was killing their friends and loved ones. The closing prayer went on and on as people wept and cried out to God. They understood that God wanted to help them work through this. He had not rejected them.

Many of the leaders had not come to the seminar that day. Later the team heard of an angry leader who had lashed out, shouting, "Do they think they are going to turn this whole thing around?" Admittedly, the problems of this world seem overwhelming, but our God specializes in turning things around. Recently, Moses told me that these skeptical leaders have made a turnaround. They are now asking the HIV/AIDS team to come again. Moses had taken the risk of inviting us and had endured the angry opposition of other leaders. His face glowed with joy as he reported the changes in their attitudes.

Satan uses his age-old tactics of fear, judgment, shame, guilt and lies to trap people in hopelessness. God forbid that his people should forget about the grace freely offered to all through Christ our Lord. God's people can turn the tide as they show compassion and forgiveness, and become instruments of healing and restoration.

Endnote
   1. *Time.* 2004. April 19, p.37.

Journaling Topic

What response do the following scriptures encourage Christians to consider in regard to social issues such as HIV/AIDS and sexual abuse? Psalm 11:3; Isaiah 61:1-3.

Idea for Prayer

Pray for church leaders in South Africa and Swaziland as they work in turning the tide of HIV/AIDS and sexual abuse in their communities.

Brenda Bagley *(2000) works in South Africa and Swaziland with Compassionate Ministries Southern Africa (CMSA), an organization she initiated in 2001, made up of a diverse group of South African and Swazi people. CMSA equips pastors and church leaders to minister to people affected and infected with HIV/AIDS. She also serves in weekly youth ministry, music ministry, hospitality ministry to overseas and local visitors and occasionally teaching in Bible colleges.*

SWEDEN
When the unexpected happens

. . . .

An Unexpected Friendship

Cheri Pierson

Known for their generous immigration policy, Sweden has given asylum to refugees from many parts of the world. Due to an expansive social system, most refugees are provided with housing, food, medical care and language classes. However, making friends with nationals is often difficult. Therefore, internationals often develop unexpected friendships with people from other cultures in their language classes.

Scripture – James 1:17
Every good and perfect gift is from above, coming down from the Father of the heavenly lights, who does not change like shifting shadows.

Story
On a bright May morning I boarded the commuter train that would take me to my first language learning class in Gothenburg, Sweden. I felt nervous as I handed the conductor my ticket, hoping he would not ask me questions since my language skills were limited to "Hello" and "Excuse me, but I'm lost." Fortunately he only took the ticket and moved on to other passengers.

Upon arrival in the city I found my way to the language school where I would spend the next year learning Swedish. As I walked up three flights of stairs, questions flooded into my mind: Would I be able to learn the language well? Would I make any friends? Would I ever be able to share the love of Christ in this foreign language?

My thoughts were interrupted when I found the classroom where a number of internationals were already seated. Two came from Africa, three from South America, two from India and one from Pakistan. No one spoke English so I sat quietly waiting for the teacher to arrive.

A young African woman came into class and sat next to me. Discovering that we both spoke English we quickly got acquainted. Adugna told me that she came from Ethiopia and was newly married. After I told her a little about myself, she asked, "Are you a Christian?" To say the least, I was surprised by her question, but I responded with an enthusiastic yes. During the break, she explained her unusual question.

Adugna had gone to Athens, Greece, to marry a man she had only met through letters. While there, she volunteered in an office for a Christian agency. Her boss, a well-known evangelist, soon led her to faith in Christ. As Adugna explained, "I was baptized and married on the same day." Adugna had to remain in Greece while her husband, who was a citizen of Sweden, went back to make arrangements for her to join him. After four months of paperwork, everything became finalized. Meanwhile her friendship with the Christians in Greece deepened and when word came for her to leave for Sweden, she hesitated. As her boss drove her to the airport he asked God to provide a friendship with a Christian woman for her in Sweden. Soon after arriving in Gothenburg, she registered for a beginning language class. Later, we figured out that it was the same day that I had registered for the same class.

As we discussed these events it became clear to us that God had a part and a purpose in our meeting each other. She asked if we could pray together and study the Bible. For the next two years we met weekly with our husbands in Bible study and our friendship deepened. Even after we moved to different cities we stayed in regular contact visiting each other as often as we could.

Adugna went on to earn a degree in dentistry from a prestigious medical school in northern Sweden. In addition, she and her husband planted more than twenty ethnic churches in Sweden and the United States. Later they moved with their four children to Nigeria where Adugna set up a dental practice among AIDS victims, offering them services when others refused to do so. Recently their mission agency assigned them to the Chicago area to work among a diverse African refugee population.

After more than twenty years apart, we find ourselves living only two miles from each other. We marvel at the good and perfect gift God has given us in our friendship and that he has brought us back together from different parts of the world.

Journaling Topic

What unexpected friendships has God given you with internationals?

Idea for Prayer

Pray for your international friends. Ask God to help you love others from various cultures.

Cheri Pierson *(1994) served with Greater Europe Mission for seventeen years. She taught English to theology students at Nordiska Bibelinstitutet and worked in women's ministries in Sweden and the Baltic countries. She also served as administrative director of the school for two years. Since 1997 she has been on the Intercultural Studies faculty of Wheaton College.*

THAILAND
When making disciples across cultures

. . . .

Yes, Lord

Dorothy Mainhood

Known as Siam until 1939, Thailand is the only southeast Asian country not taken over by a European power. Thai society has been shaped by religion, government and military might. Although industry erupted in the 1980s, Thailand historically has been an agricultural nation, filled with mountains, tropical forests and plains. Their deliciously spicy sweet and sour dishes have spread to nearly every corner of the world. Concerning religion, a small Islamic presence remains, but sculptures of Buddha and Buddhist shrines dot the landscape of Thailand.

Scripture – Matthew 28:18-20

Then Jesus came to them and said, "All authority in heaven and on earth has been given to me. Therefore go and make disciples of all nations, baptizing them in the name of the Father and of the Son and of the Holy Spirit, and teaching them to obey everything I have commanded you. And surely I am with you always, to the very end of the age."

Story

While applying to OMF, God led me, through my sister Beth, to meet and be soundly influenced by the Navigators, a Christian organization that emphasizes personal evangelism and mentoring, with the goal of seeing God raise up mature Christian workers. Strangely enough, my first term didn't look quite like the story in the pamphlet. For four years

I served as a nurse in Manorom hospital. There I learned Thai language and culture, shared in the team's evangelism among the patients and helped with a new Thai church. I had no opportunity, however, to become personally involved with the discipleship of Thai women, and I came back on my first furlough profoundly discouraged.

I told my mother that I couldn't possibly go back. "But Dorothy!" she said, "God has been leading you and he will continue to lead you." When I went to the Navigators conference, the director spoke about being a disciple—a follower of Jesus. He said, "God wants YOU to be a disciple, right where you are!" And I knew without a doubt that I was meant to follow God in Thailand, and trust him for the sense of responsibility I felt to be a "disciple-maker."

My second term of service did not begin as I had hoped, when my closest friend died of amoebic hepatitis. As I sat with her coffin in the back of the Landrover on the drive to Bangkok, I grieved her loss and wondered how she could be so sure that her work was done. She was only thirty-six. I cried out to God, "How could I know that MY work is done?" In the moment that followed, I could practically see a moving neon sign circling her coffin with these words: "Go make disciples."

For the remainder of that term I was asked to change careers from nursing to language supervising; I came back to the US to go to graduate school. Still, I had no discipling ministry. Ten years later I served in full-time language supervising, working with OMF's new church-planting team in Bangkok. There God gave me the opportunity to have Bible studies in my home. Several Thai girls stayed with me, and one American, who was new to OMF. My "class" seemed small, but for me this was a dream come true.

Alas, the dream shattered when I realized that I wanted to have a ministry of disciple-making for MYSELF. I felt devastated when the girls objected to our highly structured, somewhat pressured program and realized that they wanted to go on with God in a different way. After a heart-wrenching period of serious failure, I wanted to resign from my work with OMF's language learners to work full-time with the church. I fasted and prayed for three days, and heard God's very clear: "No, Dorothy." I said, "Yes, Lord," and came home on furlough to shed tears at each thought and mention of how my rug had been pulled out from underneath.

One time while at a supporting church in Birmingham, Alabama, I shared my story. Through the course of the testimony, I realized that I was going back to apologize to those precious girls for expecting them to follow an American style of discipleship. I decided that I would love them and let God lead me, perhaps even through them, as to how to assist in the process of their spiritual growth. "Yes, Lord," I whispered silently in my heart. When the service ended the ladies of the church handed me a handmade cross-stitch plaque that read simply, "Yes, Lord." The plaque still hangs on my office wall today.

As for the Thai girls, God granted us the grace to go through thick and thin together. Many still serve God, walking with him and bringing others—teaching them to do likewise. I finally began to understand God's dream for me—to see HIM raise up disciples, and simply let me play a part in that. He needed me to get my focus right, and he led me through the process. I'm so grateful that God helped me follow him—even though it took forty years.

Journaling Topic

What is a disciple? Are you one? Have you ever mentored someone else, helping them to grow spiritually?

Idea for Prayer

Pray that God would raise up disciples from every nation who will teach others to do the same.

Dorothy Mainhood (1987) served as a missionary with OMF International in Thailand from 1958 to 1998. She provided care for eight years as a nurse with an OMF mission hospital in Manorom, Central Thailand. After earning an MA in linguistics, Dorothy also fulfilled a position as the Thai language program supervisor—helping new missionaries gain facility in Thai to effectively live and minister there. She continues to disciple women today.

TRINIDAD
When you wonder why

. . . .

Why, God?

Diane Garvin

With its lush tropical climate, beautiful beaches and many species of birds and wildlife, Trinidad can be found just north of Venezuela, between the Caribbean Sea and the North Atlantic Ocean. The predominant philosophy of society in Trinidad can be described by Doris Day's song "Que Sera, Sera, whatever will be, will be." Their annual pre-Lenten carnival draws tourists from all over the world.

Scripture – Romans 8:28-29

And we know that in all things God works for the good of those who love him, who have been called according to his purpose. For those God foreknew he also predestined to be conformed to the likeness of his Son, that he might be the firstborn among many brothers.

Story

It was Tuesday, July 4, 12:30 p.m. A woman called my name from the street below, saying she had a message to give me. She came up to our small second-floor flat that had taken us six weeks to find. "Your husband has been in an accident. He is bleeding, but praying. Mr. Ali...well, he's dead." Needless to say, her message stunned me.

My husband John and I were ministering at the chapel, and earlier that day John had taken Mr. Ali to a nearby town to deposit that week's offerings. On their way back another car swerved into their lane while round-ing a curve and hit them head on. Both cars were traveling close to fifty miles per hour.

Immediately, my mind recalled the years of preparation that brought me to this point. It was our first missionary assignment. We had delayed starting a family in order to finish school and get to the field. After spending several years raising support—working all summer painting houses inside and out to raise our outgoing expenses, and struggling for a year to learn Spanish—we were directed to another field assignment. Now just six months in Trinidad, and this accident occurs. "God, what on earth are you doing?" I asked. Gently, he reminded me of Romans 8:28.

John's injuries were extensive—too extensive for the hospital in our city to manage. So for the next ten days I tried to arrange a flight back to the United States. Questions periodically bounced around in my mind: Didn't we meet your criteria? Didn't we love you more than anything—even more than each other? Weren't we called to be here? I thought I knew the answers, but I still found myself asking, "Why God? Why?"

"What will be, will be." That was the philosophy of the hospital medical personnel when they explained why they did nothing to ease John's pain. Upon arrival at the hospital he lay on a steel table for nearly eight hours with broken ribs, a punctured lung, a severely dislocated hip and lacerated knees, without any pain medicine or clean-up. Multiple x-rays had been taken, but when he went to the ward, they mistakenly placed the cast on his left ankle—an old high school football injury. Then he was given no oxygen to ease the strain in his punctured lung. Dealing with the delays, having to watch my husband suffer and grieving over the death of Mr. Ali all proved difficult, but what made it more so was the stark fact that God remained silent—leaving all my questions unanswered.

A month after we arrived back in the US I sat next to John's bed reading Romans 8. It was then that God opened my eyes to see the verse that follows 28. Verse 29 reads, "For those God foreknew he also predestined to become conformed to the likeness of his Son, that he might be the first-born among many brothers."

I'll never forget the clarity of God's message to me that day. I had been chosen by God to go through this suffering, in order to be more like Jesus.

My loving Father had a plan, and it was a good plan. Being like Jesus is always good, and I am secure in him. Although John underwent numerous surgeries and faced serious health challenges over the next twenty-four years of his life I never asked God "Why?" again. I knew from the depths of my being that in Jesus everything made sense. It would all be okay.

Journaling Topic

How do I see adversity in my life? Do I believe that God's call pertains only to a place, a time or a set of circumstances? Why or why not?

Idea for Prayer

Pray for the safety of missionaries around the globe. Pray for their strength and resilience to endure and persevere.

Diane Garvin (1988) served with her husband in Trinidad and, later, in the Republic of South Africa, planting churches among Asian Indians. Since 1988 she has been employed at the Billy Graham Center, and is currently the coordinator for the Billy Graham Center Scholarship Program.

UNITED STATES
When home is far away

. . . .

Where is My Home?

Mary Cerutti

From roaring metropolises to rolling hills, from the tropical climate of Florida to the chilly weather of Alaska—the landscape of the United States varies greatly. This great superpower of the world has been coined "the melting pot"—referring to its high rate of national immigration. From all over the world, people come to the US in hopes of finding a better life for themselves and for their families. Multiple aid organizations work with displaced people who find themselves within the borders of North America, as well as those trying to finalize their citizenship.

Scripture – John 14: 2-4

In my Father's house are many rooms; if it were not so, I would have told you. I am going there to prepare a place for you...I will come back and take you to be with me that you also may be where I am. You know the way to the place where I am going.

Story

Before refugees come to the United States they may spend months, years or even decades in a refugee camp. This place temporarily forms their "home." The camps accommodate anywhere from a few thousand to hundreds of thousands of people. The sites are usually located on the edges of towns or cities. While some seem well organized, others become huge haphazard collections of makeshift shelters made of anything from sticks and plastic sheeting to bamboo huts and tents formed of plastic. Aid workers strive to provide at least one tap of water for every 250 people, and a "home-cooked" meal is often one of corn, grains, beans, oil, sugar and salt—the basic ingredients provided by relief agencies. If, however, little food is available or the number of displaced people is too massive, they instead receive biscuits that contain enough nutrients to last an entire day.

"Home" is where we usually want to be. We sing songs such as "Take Me Home Country Roads" and "Home on the Range," and display plaques with phrases like "Home Is Where the Heart Is" and "Home Sweet Home." While these songs may induce happy thoughts of nostalgia for some Americans, for many refugees "home" is a place they will never see again. Although their stories vary, their homeland is often a place of persecution, war and turmoil, but still they long to return. Like all of us, "home" often consists of the people that they love and miss the most. Teaching English to refugees, I earned the privilege of hearing a number of their stories, but three women with their stories remain prominent in my mind.

Mabintz was a young woman from Sierra Leone. One day at age seventeen, Mabintz came home from school to find all of her family had disappeared. People all around her ran to buses nearby with signs that told her they were traveling to Nigeria. Rebels rampaged through the area, kidnapping, raping and killing people; she had no choice but to board a bus and leave her home. Although she believes that her family is still alive, she has not seen them since that day.

Mira, a woman in her fifties, tells me in broken English that she lived a good life in her homeland of Bosnia. She worked as a cashier, and her family busied themselves with constructing a new home when suddenly war broke out. Her family fled to Belgrade, but she was forced to leave her husband behind. For eight months they waited for him to get the necessary paperwork and join them. In spite of all this Mira says that her greatest challenge in her new "home" has been learning English.

Hannah is a woman I tutored in English. After completing high school in Ethiopia, she traveled to the Czech Republic to study engineering on a scholarship. While at the college she participated in a political organization that opposed the military leaders of Ethiopia. She joined the organization because she believed in what they stood for. Later she discovered the cost of her enlistment. She found that any student associated with this organization would be imprisoned upon their return to Ethiopia.

In desperation she applied for political asylum in the United States. Since then Hannah and I have become good friends—sharing everything from recipes to ideas for raising our young children. I've seen her tears as she talks about missing her mom, and the fact that her mother has not seen either of her children, who were both born in the United States.

These three women represent others who miss their homeland and their family. In my conversations with refugees I have learned that one way to help meet their needs is to take time to be a friend and develop a lasting relationship. In sharing our lives with those far away from home, we can bring some sense of home and hope to their present lives. And hearing their stories makes me appreciate so much more my own home and family.

Recently my husband and I adopted our daughter from China. I remember leaving China and walking up to the security line at the Guangzhou airport when, suddenly, I began to sob uncontrollably. I realized that I felt sad about taking our new one-year-old daughter from her country, her people and her home. My prayer is that we can provide a good home for her and develop relationships with other Chinese people to help our daughter connect with her own culture. But above all, my prayer for my daughter, as well as every displaced person that I meet, is that they will find their eternal home in heaven.

Journaling Topic

How can I reach out to someone far from home? How can I be more inviting to those who are lonely and far from family and friends?

Idea for Prayer

Pray for agencies that resettle thousands of refugees like Mabintz, Mira and Hannah in the United States every year. Pray for more churches and host families to welcome them into their fellowship and homes.

Mary Cerutti (2004) committed more than ten years to the business world in various Human Resource management positions. Currently she teaches English to adult refugees and immigrants through a resettlement agency. Mary is married and has an adopted daughter, Michelle, from China.

UNITED STATES
When looking for direction

. . . .

Leaning In and Pressing On

Brooke Peters

Scripture – Jeremiah 29:11
"For I know the plans I have for you," declares the Lord, "plans to prosper you and not to harm you, plans to give you hope and a future."

Story

I have desired to hear stories about women in my stage of life and preparation for the field so that I might discern my own next steps and understand my calling, but I have yet to find many such recorded experiences. I have been overseas on different short-term stints: two weeks, two months, ten months and studied missions and intercultural studies with experienced missionaries. Rubbing shoulders with fellow pilgrims on these trips has helped me to better understand the Lord's purposes for the nations, and fueled my desire to be a part of spreading his glory to areas that offer increased opportunities. Still, I find that the "next steps" are not as easy to make as I thought they would be.

The actual walking out of the "next steps" appears to be complex. Perhaps this is in part because of my personality, which looks at all possibilities and wants to know all the facts, but I think the answer lies more in realizing the spiritual battle that rages on unseen. How subtle are the lures of the one who seeks to steal, kill and destroy (John 10). In writing this I hope to offer others the companionship I've sought—to be someone to relate to and help others know they don't stand alone in their struggles, questions and confusion.

In my own life I have seen this spiritual battle wage through a deluge of conflicting thoughts; it is as though I am seeing two completely different worlds. The first vision reveals me, here in the US with a family, ministering through my job or to my children. The other vision shows me sharing the love of Jesus with those who live on the margins of society, where little access exists to the Word or a body of believers. But when I'm honest about my inabilities, I wonder if I can handle the pressure that will come. I do not condemn myself for these thoughts—I know that the Lord would still love me, teach me and use me in any situation.

Despite some doubts, something nudges me forward in the direction of the second picture. The purpose and love in God's Word reveals the story of an intimate God choosing a people for himself and making a way for all nations to be part of this beloved family. The wrestling lessens when I answer these questions for myself. Do I believe that God is able to do "immeasurably more than all we ask or imagine" (Eph. 3:20)? Will I trust that his "grace is sufficient" (2 Cor. 12:9)? Do I love my comfort more than I love him and more than the spreading of his glory? Am I willing to die to myself, even when I do not know the specifics of what that means, or what that might look like (Gal. 2:20)? Although this time of discerning and deciding has been trying, it has also been soothing for it has purified my heart and my motives.

It is too easy to let my eyes turn inward. My thoughts find rest in my own circumstances and unanswered questions. But I am not content to stay there any longer. When I refocus on God, the Blessed Trinity of Father, Son and Holy Spirit—on the Father, who purposed to make himself known in all the world; on Jesus, who had no sin but became our sin; on the Holy Spirit, who leads us in truth, counsels us and empowers us—then I feel strengthened in faith and able to go forward. I am moved by and grateful for the saints of the past, in both biblical times and since—Paul, Augustine, Bonhoeffer, Mother Teresa and even present-day saints—those who urge us on and believe in the One who lives in the unseen, yet affects the seen. They cry out for us to press on in "being sure of what we hope for and certain of what we do not see" (Heb. 11:1).

May God encourage you today to rest in his intimate love for you—to see the potential that lies beyond the visible, and to go forth to spread the glory of the One who is worthy.

Journaling Topic

What is God calling me to do? How am I intentionally seeking his will for my life?

Idea for Prayer

Pray for those currently in training for the mission field. Pray that they would be well equipped for their assignment.

Brooke Peters *(2002) works full-time and volunteers in an international student ministry. There she sorts through information about organizations and is in the midst of deciding whether to serve long-term overseas. She has been a cross-cultural worker in several different contexts, most recently Thailand where she worked with university students. This story reflects her thoughts as she seeks God's will for the next stage of her life.*

UNITED STATES

When others are hurting

. . . .

The Spirit's Song of Healing

Heather Kirsten Pancake

Riverwoods Christian Center, Illinois, USA

A non-profit, support-based ministry, Riverwoods is located along the Fox River in a suburb of Chicago, Illinois. Over seven hundred youth come through their eight-week summer camp programs. The youth who attend come from families with incomes below the poverty line. Most attend schools in poor educational systems and live in homes surrounded by gangs, drugs, theft, abuse, violence and social injustice. At Riverwoods, water and trees replace pavement and low-income housing developments, screams of laughter and camp activities replace the life of the street, and the message of the gospel of Jesus Christ is not only preached, but lived.

Scripture – Isaiah 57:18-19

"I have seen his ways, but I will heal him; I will guide him and restore comfort to him, creating praise on the lips of the mourners in Israel. Peace, peace to those far and near," says the Lord. "And I will heal them."

Story

Nikki sat across from me, vulnerable and wide-eyed. She had just finished telling me more of her story. My heart went out to her for it seemed clear that she overflowed with insecurity and fear. She so bravely peeled away the layers and walls around her heart, only to unveil the raw and bleeding wounds still fresh after years of victimization, abuse and sin. I took a moment to look silently in those wide eyes. I did not mean to smile or say a word, but simply to whisper from my heart to hers that she was loved. I wanted her to know that in the most vulnerable opening of secret places, I would not reject her or laugh at her pain.

Her father had abused her physically and emotionally by angrily yelling at her and demanding she behave just as he commanded. He incited a horrifying fear in her. Nikki's mother was herself a deeply wounded woman due to an abortion she had undergone. She had been raped and abandoned as a young girl. On top of that Nikki's mother had fights with her husband—one ending in a struggle to breathe as he held her up on the wall by her neck. Her mother was so caught up and overwhelmed with getting through each day that she subjected Nikki to the abuse of neglect.

Nikki also had to deal with two brothers, one who threatened her with a butcher knife and terrified her by pounding her bedroom door. She locked it and fiercely leaned all her bodyweight against it to keep him from hitting her. Her other brother protected her somewhat, yet still fought with her.

Then a time came when they watched a graphic R-rated movie with their father, and he used her to satisfy his body's reaction to the film. She had been taken advantage of sexually by numerous other males since the tender age of five. They stole her innocence and instilled lies deep within her precious childlike heart. I continued to look intensely into her eyes. I wanted to reach into the dark places of her soul and communicate a love that she had never experienced before.

After the moments locked in eye contact, I was surprised to find no words to speak; no prayers to pray. Instead, I opened my guitar case, closed my eyes and began to listen to the Spirit sing his truth through my fingers and my voice. The music resounded throughout the high ceilings of my living room. As Nikki listened, the last of her walls crumbled into pieces. Tears flowed freely, and her sobs sounded to the music as the Spirit reached in and touched those deep, unveiled places of her heart and soul. He spoke truth to her. She is his beloved child; she is forgiven and pure in him. She is washed and clothed in white before his throne. His love for her is unconditional, and his promise of healing, restoration and new life is assured.

As I listened to the promptings in my spirit, I knew unfathomable peace. The healer showed me which song to sing as he lovingly worked in Nikki's heart; I simply strummed along—only an accompanist to the master composer. I knew that he was the one singing the song as he cradled her in his arms of unfailing love. This song was his song to Nikki, and to so many of us who have been wounded. In the words of DJ Butler, "I will change your name; You shall no longer be called wounded, outcast, lonely or afraid. I will change your name; Your new name shall be confidence, joyfulness, overcoming one, faithfulness, friend of God, one who seeks my face."

In the quietness of the presence of the Lord I understood that the hope we each look for, wide-eyed and vulnerable, is found only in the Lord Jesus Christ. His song of healing and love waits for our hearts to open, in trust, to him.

Journaling Topic

What wounds are you still guarding within your heart? Will you open those places and invite the healer in this moment?

Idea for Prayer

Pray for the precious children who suffer from childhood abuse, that they will come to intimately know the One who promises to bring them healing and peace. Pray also for adults still struggling with unconfessed sins and scars of their past.

Heather Kirsten Pancake (2003) served for one year as Camp Program Manager at Riverwoods Christian Center. She graduated from Wheaton College in 2000 with a BA in Christian Education and Ministry, as well as a BA in Bible/Theology. Upon graduation, she moved down to central Mexico to serve as a missionary with Christ For Children International before moving back to the United States to earn her MA in Intercultural Studies, and a Certificate in Leadership and Camp Ministry, from Wheaton College in August 2003.

UNITED STATES

When you move beyond
your comfort zone

. . . .

Sarah

Dawn Herzog Jewell

Sarah comes from the country of Liberia which is located in Northern Africa, bordering the Mediterranean Sea. The nation has a Mediterranean climate along the coast, but an extreme desert climate inland.

Scripture – Luke 10:29b
...so he asked Jesus, "And who is my neighbor?"

Story

God blew Sarah Kollie into my life two Septembers ago, when crimson began seeping into the maple trees of Chicago's western suburbs. Sarah's mother, father and four younger sisters survived civil war in Liberia. They had landed at O'Hare Airport nine months earlier, clutching each other and the white plastic "Office of Migration" bags that marked them as refugees.

I was single, twenty-eight and recently transplanted from Seattle's familiar mountain peaks to the flatlands of Wheaton, Illinois, for work. I vaguely grasped that my daily world revolved around me. I was looking for a ticket off the merry-go-round ride for narcissistic singles.

I nervously climbed the dirty, carpeted staircase in Glendale Village Apartments the first time on a rainy September evening. The cracked plywood door of #206 swung open and a man's deep accented voice ushered me in.

The apartment seemed gloomier than the hallway. Heavy curtains trapped all outdoor light and dark couches nearly hid the faces of the Kollie family. My eyes adjusted and Sarah's father Boima clasped my hand firmly. "How are you?" he asked, grinning and pointing to a wide-eyed girl in blue denim overalls. Sarah smiled shyly, her caramel colored face lighting up. Her hair was sectioned into ten braided pigtails.

"Sarah needs to learn to read and write. I will be very glad, very glad, if you can teach her," Boima said. "She needs an education, to go to college. If you have education in this country, you can do anything."

Me? All I wanted was a friendly cultural exchange—to learn to say "thank you" in a new language, to try some exotic ethnic cuisine and teach newcomers how to carve pumpkins. I shuddered at shouldering responsibility for a college education. "I'll try," I said.

That Saturday I muddled through literacy books at the local Learning Express store, grabbing cheap blue phonics workbooks. I checked out with four books and a packet of "good job!" stickers for $15.

The next Wednesday evening I returned to #206. Sarah connected a bat with the letter "b." We progressed to "g" and giraffe while fighting off Sarah's 5-year-old sister Nasu. Did I have to baby-sit besides tutor an illiterate college-bound fourth-grader? "Lord, give me patience," I prayed.

I was eager to introduce Sarah to the world beyond her cramped apartment and ready for a reprieve from her clutching sister's hands. On Saturday morning we piled into my little red Geo Metro convertible for Kline Creek Farm. We had just passed the Jewel supermarket when Sarah blurted, "My father doesn't care about me. All he cares about is my schoolwork. He doesn't take me anywhere fun."

"I think he loves you and that's why he cares about your schoolwork," I said.

"Yeah, but he doesn't do anything with us, I don't like him," she said.

"I didn't like how my father treated my mother when I was growing up," I said. "He always yelled."

"Really?" Sarah said quietly. My pain comforted her. Her father wasn't unique in his failings.

That day I began to appreciate our bond as more than tutor and student. My transient life developed purpose—I had more to offer Sarah than ABCs.

Sarah had to prove her courage quickly on Ruskin Elementary's blacktop playground. One lunch recess three bullies circled Sarah and her friend Marcella. "Give us your money," one fifth-grader demanded, "or we'll beat you up."

"We don't have any money, leave us alone," Sarah yelled.

"Then steal some from your parents," another boy demanded, shoving Marcella to the blacktop.

"No!" Sarah jumped on the startled boy and pounded on his chest until he scrambled up and fled with his friends.

"Did you tell your father?" I asked.

"No," Sarah said, "then he'd talk to the principal and I'd get in trouble."

Forces beyond Sarah's control had forced her family to flee their home and country. She chose to fight for what she could change. I thirsted for a dollop of her fierceness to boost my own fear of conflict. A few days later she reported justice—the boys were suspended.

Sarah's battlefield raged on the home front, too. "My mom and dad are arguing a lot. I don't want them to divorce," Sarah confided to me as we strolled around her block one windy Sunday afternoon.

"Neither do I," I said. "But marriage is hard and sometimes parents have a lot of problems. It's not your fault. They still love you." I reached for her hand, but Sarah was chewing her nails in distress. "I can't help it," she said.

A few weeks later Sarah's mother answered the phone. "Last night Sarah spoke to her father and me. 'God doesn't like you when you fight,' Sarah told us. Sarah has never said anything like this before to us." Her mother's voice filled with awe and respect. Pride and wonder swept through me.

Sarah's parents still argue. Her father lost his job last summer. "We don't have quarters for laundry today," she told me last weekend. But Sarah and her family are building a new life in the US. I still dread her dim, smoky apartment and the cockroaches that crawl across the kitchen counter, but Sarah reminds me that I am needed beyond my comfortable church socials and graduate school classes. More is required of me in Sarah's world.

Journaling Topic

Think of the people in your life. Are there needs beyond the surface that you could help with such as Dawn did with Sara?

Idea for Prayer

Pray for recent refugees that they would find the supportive relationships to help with language learning and everyday issues.

Dawn Herzog Jewell *(2004) is publications and training manager for Media Associates International, a ministry that equips Christian publishers, editors and writers around the world. Her role with MAI combines her interests in writing/editing, training leaders and reaching nations for Christ. She is also a freelance missions writer.*

ZAMBIA
When risks are inevitable

. . . .

We Will Fear No Evil

Shelli Martin and Holly VanSciver

Zambia lies on the Central African Plateau at the southern end of the Great Rift Valley. Like most African countries, its inhabitants love filling the air with the heavily rhythmic music, traditional of the culture. Although poor in monetary wealth, the country teems with nature and wildlife. Amidst the Muchinga mountains and the earth's biggest waterfall live approximately thirty-five ethnic groups and seventy different tribes—none of which is dominant. They feel proud of their tribal harmony.

Scripture – Psalm 91: 4
He will cover you with his feathers, and under his wings you will find refuge; his faithfulness will be your shield and rampart.

Story
My roommate Holly and I work in Lusaka, the capital of Zambia. As Community Health Facilitator with World Hope International, I work primarily with youth, educating them in the biblical approach to the issues surrounding HIV/AIDS through seminars, conferences and partnership with the Evangelical Fellowship of Zambia (EFZ).

The fight against AIDS wages intensely because the problem runs deep and wide culturally. One can sense the spiritual battle raging around us. Satan has blinded the eyes of so many to the truth about this disease;

carelessness runs rampant. The youth are constantly bombarded with the stress of personal anger and jealousy or peer pressures. So every night before bed, I pray for my own safety and the safety of my friends—that a protective canopy would be placed over our property and home; that we would be covered by the blood of Jesus, and experience his protection. Danger has come close to us, but it has not yet touched us and we don't take this for granted.

God surprised us in the midst of this when the idea of a church plant blossomed and came to fruition. Beginning in one of the most stigmatized shantytowns on the edge of Lusaka, we spent our Saturdays teaching a Bible study there, followed by a church service on Sunday, held outside someone's home on a straw mat under a papaya tree.

We face many challenges during our meetings. The place is known for thievery and extreme poverty. There are more taverns (with locally-brewed beer) than churches, so we must suit up in spiritual armor before each encounter. One day a woman came to the group and demonic spirits began to manifest themselves through her. Others quickly moved away in fear, but Holly and I laid our hands on the woman and began to pray. Although the demonic activity subsided, the woman has not yet been delivered. We pray that God will free her from spiritual torment and bondage.

The woman has never returned to the church (because of social embarrassment), but the experience gave us an opportunity to teach the other women about the power of God. Although fear resides in this place, God retains authority over Satan, his demons and even fear itself. In Zambia many respond to fear by running away—taking what they think is the "easy" way out. They surrender instead of standing firm in Christ. Holly and I know the victor, and our lives have been easy compared to those of the people we serve.

Journaling Topic

How do we minister to people who struggle with poverty, sin, demon possession or tragic loss? What is spiritual warfare? How do we prepare ourselves for it?

Idea for Prayer

Pray that God would raise up strong and faithful prayer warriors for Zambia. Pray for new believers and miracles. Pray for political and economic stability.

Shelli Martin *(2001) cares for orphans affected by HIV/AIDS as a Community Health Facilitator with World Hope International in Lusaka, Zambia. Along with* **Holly Van-Sciver** *(2002), she planted a church in a shanty town on the edge of Lusaka.*

Journaling Notes

Journaling Notes

Journaling Notes

Journaling Notes

Journaling Notes

Journaling Notes

DATE DUE